10/94

SECRET DEMOCRACY
Civil Liberties vs. The National Security State

Gary E. McCuen

IDEAS IN CONFLICT SERIES

GEM
Gary McCuen
publications inc.
502 Second Street
Hudson, Wisconsin 54016
Phone (715) 386-7113

All rights reserved. No part of this book may be reproduced or stored by any means without prior permission from the copyright owner.

Illustration & photo credits

Don Carlton 13, Duffy 29, Horsey 106, Dan Hubig 88, Doug MacGregor 20, Craig MacIntosh 49, *The Militant* 122, Eleanor Mill 60, H. Payne 85, 111, Renault 79, David Seavey 38, 94, Carol*Simpson 142, John Trever 68, Edd Uluschak 116, Richard Wright 44, 55, 150. Cover illustration by Ron Swanson.

©1990 by Gary E. McCuen Publications, Inc.
502 Second Street, Hudson, Wisconsin 54016
(715) 386-7113
International Standard Book Number
0-86596-074-7
Printed in the United States of America

CONTENTS

Ideas in Conflict   6

CHAPTER 1   SECRECY AND DEMOCRACY: HISTORICAL OVERVIEW

1. THE THREAT TO CIVIL LIBERTIES   9
   John Shattuck

2. SECRECY AND DEMOCRACY ARE COMPATIBLE   16
   Mary C. Lawton

CHAPTER 2   TERRORISM, DRUGS, AND THE CIA

3. PROMOTING VIOLENCE: THE DARK SIDE OF U.S. FOREIGN POLICY   25
   John Stockwell

4. PROTECTING DEMOCRACY: SECRECY AND NATIONAL SECURITY IN FOREIGN AFFAIRS   34
   George A. Carver, Jr.

5. THE CIA WAS INVOLVED IN DRUG TRADE   41
   Daniel Siegel and Jenny Yancey

6. NO DRUG SMUGGLING TOOK PLACE   46
   Robert A. Bermingham

7. TERRORISM THREATENS U.S. SECURITY   51
   Richard H. Shultz, Jr.

8. OUR DOUBLE STANDARD ON TERRORISM   57
   Jeff Cohen

CHAPTER 3 COVERT ACTION AND FOREIGN AFFAIRS

9. THE CASE AGAINST COVERT ACTION 64
   Clark M. Clifford

10. THE CASE FOR COVERT ACTION 70
    George A. Carver, Jr.

11. THE SECRET CONSPIRACY BEHIND IRAN/CONTRAGATE 75
    The Christic Institute

12. NO CONSPIRACY EXISTED 81
    Cliff Kincaid

CHAPTER 4 DOMESTIC SPYING AND POLITICAL DISSENT

13. THE FBI'S CRIMINAL BEHAVIOR 90
    Mike Zielinski

14. THE FBI WAS RIGHT ABOUT CISPES 97
    Human Events

15. SPYING ON THE CHURCHES: THE POINT 102
    Garrett Brown

16. SPYING ON THE CHURCHES: THE COUNTERPOINT 108
    James P. Turner

17. TARGETING THE SOCIALIST WORKERS PARTY 112
    Political Rights Defense Fund

18. THE CASE AGAINST THE SOCIALIST WORKERS PARTY 118
    Gary B. McDaniel

CHAPTER 5 COVERT ACTION AND INTELLIGENCE: IDEAS IN CONFLICT

19. MASSIVE CIVIL LIBERTIES VIOLATIONS 126
    Herman Schwartz

20. PRESENT LAWS PROTECT LIBERTY 133
    William H. Webster

21. FORSAKING DEMOCRACY: 138
    THE COLD WAR AND COVERT ACTION
    Eric Black

22. PROTECTING DEMOCRACY: 146
    INTELLIGENCE AND COVERT ACTIONS IN HISTORY
    The Minority Report of the Iran-Contra Affair

Appendix: Definition of Key Terms 156
Bibliography: Congress and Intelligence Policy 159

REASONING SKILL DEVELOPMENT

These activities may be used as individualized study guides for students in libraries and resource centers or as discussion catalysts in small group and classroom discussions.

1. What Is Editorial Bias? 22
2. Recognizing Author's Point of View 62
3. Interpreting Editorial Cartoons 87
4. Examining Counterpoints 123
5. What Is Political Bias? 153

IDEAS in CONFLICT®

This series features ideas in conflict on political, social and moral issues. It presents counterpoints, debates, opinions, commentary and analysis for use in libraries and classrooms. Each title in the series uses one or more of the following basic elements:

Introductions that present an issue overview giving historic background and/or a description of the controversy.

Counterpoints and debates carefully chosen from publications, books, and position papers on the political right and left to help librarians and teachers respond to requests that treatment of public issues be fair and balanced.

Symposiums and forums that go beyond debates that can polarize and oversimplify. These present commentary from across the political spectrum that reflect how complex issues attract many shades of opinion.

A *global* emphasis with foreign perspectives and surveys on various moral questions and political issues that will help readers to place subject matter in a less culture-bound and ethno-centric frame of reference. In an ever shrinking and interdependent world, understanding and cooperation are essential. Many issues are global in nature and can be effectively dealt with only by common efforts and international understanding.

Reasoning skill study guides and discussion activities provide ready made tools for helping with critical reading and evaluation of content. The guides and activities deal with one or more of the following:

RECOGNIZING AUTHOR'S POINT OF VIEW

INTERPRETING EDITORIAL CARTOONS

VALUES IN CONFLICT

WHAT IS EDITORIAL BIAS?

WHAT IS SEX BIAS?
WHAT IS POLITICAL BIAS?
WHAT IS ETHNOCENTRIC BIAS?
WHAT IS RACE BIAS?
WHAT IS RELIGIOUS BIAS?

*From across **the political spectrum** varied sources are presented for research projects and classroom discussions. Diverse opinions in the series come from magazines, newspapers, syndicated columnists, books, political speeches, foreign nations, and position papers by corporations and non-profit institutions.*

About the Editor

Gary E. McCuen is an editor and publisher of anthologies for public libraries and curriculum materials for schools. Over the past 19 years his publications of over 200 titles have specialized in social, moral and political conflict. They include books, pamphlets, cassettes, tabloids, filmstrips and simulation games, many of them designed from his curriculums during 11 years of teaching junior and senior high school social studies. At present he is the editor and publisher of the *Ideas in Conflict* series and the *Editorial Forum* series.

CHAPTER 1

SECRECY AND DEMOCRACY: HISTORICAL OVERVIEW

1. THE THREAT TO CIVIL LIBERTIES 9
   John Shattuck

2. SECRECY AND DEMOCRACY ARE COMPATIBLE 16
   Mary C. Lawton

READING
1
SECRECY AND DEMOCRACY

THE THREAT TO CIVIL LIBERTIES

John Shattuck

John Shattuck presented the following testimony in his capacity as vice president for Government, Community, and Public Affairs for Harvard University.

Points to Consider:

1. Describe the two key principles established in the Pentagon Papers decision.
2. How can certain information be "born classified"?
3. Why was the Supreme Court's ruling in the national security wiretap case considered significant?
4. What does the author mean when he says we "have drifted into a state of permanent emergency that has no immediate context"?

Excerpted from the testimony of John Shattuck before the House Subcommittee on Courts, Civil Liberties, and the Administration of Justice of the House Committee on the Judiciary, September 26, 1984.

Without clearly defining what we mean by national security, we have turned it into a talisman to ward off any evil that might befall us as a nation.

A central theme of these hearings has been the threat to civil liberties from increasingly broad claims of national security asserted by the President and other officials of the executive branch. These assertions have become especially sweeping during the Reagan Administration—as in the case of the news blackout of the Grenada invasion, the promulgation of a presidential directive imposing lifetime censorship on government employees handling classified information, the use of export controls to limit the publication of scientific research, and many other examples brought out in these hearings. While the Reagan Administration has been particularly active in making claims of national security to curtail civil liberties, its policies are the culmination of a long trend which began after World War II and accelerated during the Nixon Administration.

National Security and Civil Liberties

Nowhere is this more evident than in the areas of censorship and electronic surveillance. Here the Nixon Administration stands out from other recent presidencies only because of the fate of its principal, not because its policies presented a unique threat to civil liberties. In fact, the development of a law of national security secrecy and surveillance, and its steady erosion of the First and Fourth Amendments, has accelerated in the post-Watergate era.

Until 1971 the national security secrecy system had been created and maintained by the executive branch alone. The only law establishing the system was a series of executive orders issued by Presidents Truman, Eisenhower, Kennedy, and Nixon. There were security clearances and investigations in many government agencies, and millions of pages of classified documents. But there was no systematic enforcement of secrecy and no stamp of approval by the courts or the Congress. All that began to change when the Nixon Administration went to court in May 1971 to try to block the *New York Times* from publishing the Pentagon Papers. Although the case is widely regarded as a victory for freedom of the press, the Pentagon papers litigation actually set in motion the development of a formal law of national security secrecy.

National Security Secrecy

In its Pentagon Papers decision, the Supreme Court abandoned the longstanding limitation of prior restraints to narrow wartime circumstances. The pivotal concurring opinions of Justices Stewart and White for the first time generalized the category of information subject to prior restraint and recognized the authority of Congress to legislate in this sensitive constitutional territory. After the dust had settled, the Nixon Administration and its successors began to claim that the Pentagon Papers decision had actually established two key principles in a new law of secrecy: first, that the government can block publication of information if its disclosure will "surely result in direct, immediate, and irreparable damage to the nation," as Justice Stewart put it; and second, that if Congress passes a statute authorizing prior restraint, the standard for obtaining an injunction to stop publication can be even lower.

The cat was out of the bag. A succession of post-Watergate cases transformed it into a tiger with a ravenous appetite for the First Amendment. The most spectacular prior restraints to be imposed in the period after the Pentagon Papers decision involved former employees of the CIA whose writings the government claimed the right to censor. The Victor Marchetti and Frank Snepp decisions established the legal principle that the CIA, and presumably other government agencies as well, can bar a current or former employee from publishing "any information or material relating to the agency, its activities or intelligence activities generally, either during or after the term of [his or her] employment... without specific prior approval of the agency." This new principle was based on the law of contract—if you work for an agency that operated within the national security secrecy system, your employment contract obligates you to waive permanently your First Amendment rights to speak and publish without prior restraint.

Certain Information Can Be "Born Classified"

Closely paralleling the growth of contract secrecy was the development of a legal theory that certain information can be "born classified." In 1979 the Justice Department moved against the *Progressive* magazine in an effort to block it from publishing information that was already in the public domain. The *Progressive* case involved an article written about the hydrogen bomb based on information obtained by its author, Howard Morland, from studying government publications. In its effort to obtain an injunction, the government argued that information about atomic weapons is "born classified" and can be restricted under the Atomic Energy Act whether or not its disclosure would meet the Pentagon Papers standard. Although the government eventually abandoned the *Progressive* case when it became clear that the information in Morland's article was not secret, the theory put forward by the Justice Department was that there are whole categories of "dangerous information" that are beyond the reach of the First Amendment.

Three years later, in 1982, the Reagan Administration began using this same theory in its well publicized effort to persuade academic scientists to submit certain categories of research plans to the government for clearance. . . .

Conducting Warrantless Wiretaps

Like the law of secrecy, the law of national security surveillance has evolved from bold presidential assertions of power to an extensive authority set forth in judicial decisions and congressional enactment. Every president since Franklin Roosevelt has claimed the power to conduct warrantless wiretapping of foreign governments. But it was the Nixon Administration which put forward the most sweeping claims in this area, and sought to have them approved by the courts.

In a series of cases beginning in 1969, the Nixon Administration argued that it had an inherent power to disregard the Fourth Amendment warrant requirement whenever it conducted wiretaps or physical searches of persons or groups believed to be a threat to the national security. In the first such case to reach the appellate level, this argument was rejected by both the Sixth Circuit Court of Appeals and a unanimous Supreme Court in 1972. Like the Pentagon papers decision, however, the Court's ruling in the national security wiretap case was also significant for what it did not decide. Since the wiretap at issue had been installed on a domestic organization with no connections to any foreign power, the Court left open the possibility that warrantless surveillance of a person or group with "foreign ties" would be legal.

The political turmoil in the Nixon White House obscured the steady development of a new law of national security surveillance. Taking its cue from the Supreme Court's 1972 wiretap decision, the law began to focus on the elusive concept of "foreign agency." Since the Court had held that the Fourth Amendment only barred warrantless national security surveillance of domestic targets, suspected agents of a foreign power were presumed to be beyond its reach. Ironically, this distinction

NCR/Don Carlton.

established a legal rationale for much of the surveillance that had been condemned in the Nixon era. One example was the CIA's program of spying on the anti-Vietnam War movement, "Operation CHAOS." This was a surveillance effort to ferret out links between the leaders of the peace movement and foreign governments. Although no such links were ever established, the program resulted in the creation of CIA files on more than 300,000 domestic activists participating in activities that had been under suspicion for having a foreign stimulus.

A Foreign Security Loophole

The Ford, Carter, and Reagan administrations have all claimed, in a series of executive orders, that undefined foreign agent surveillance is beyond the reach of the Fourth Amendment. These executive orders have been issued with much public fanfare proclaiming the "rule of law" over the "intelligence abuses" of the Watergate era. At the same time, however, the orders have been broadly drafted to fit the needs of national security, regardless of their impact on civil liberties. The Reagan order represents the culmination of this process. It goes far beyond the "foreign agent" approach of the Carter Administration and authorizes the CIA to conduct general surveillance of anyone inside the United States who may be in possession of "significant foreign intelligence," such as journalists or academics or businessmen returning from trips overseas. It also authorizes the CIA to conduct undefined covert operations inside the United States so long as they are not "intended to influence the political process, public opinion, policies or the media." . . .

A State of Permanent Emergency

What is most remarkable about all this is that we seem to have drifted into a state of permanent emergency that has no immediate context. We do not know what the emergency is or how long it will last. We do not even have a clear understanding of its impact on our system of liberty, since we have been conditioned to accept the view that the rule of law often requires individual liberty to yield to claims of security under certain limited circumstances. In fact, we do not even think of ourselves as living in a state of emergency. On the contrary, we believe that a general suspension of liberty happens only in other countries. . . .

Is the United States becoming such a country? Without clearly defining what we mean by national security, we have turned it into a talisman to ward off any evil that might befall us as a nation. It is disturbing, but not surprising, therefore, that the Reagan Administration turned the CIA loose to spy on Americans and conduct "covert actions" inside the U.S.; created a presumption that all government information about foreign or military affairs can be withheld from the public; pardoned FBI officials who supervised criminal burglaries as heroes in a war against terrorism; and mounted a campaign for official censorship of scientific research.

A Simple Question

There is a simple question that we must ask ourselves as we look at these recent developments and the long history of national security maneuvers that preceded them: where does the Constitution fit in? National security is what protects us from our adversaries, but the Constitution and the Bill of Rights are what distinguish us from them. The question, of course, is not just one of law. We must decide what we mean by national security and whether its protection would be allowed to blur our principal distinguishing features as a nation. "Liberty lies in the hearts of all men," Judge Learned Hand said in a famous speech delivered during a time of grave national danger, in 1943. "When it dies there, no constitution, no law, no court can save it." Judge Hand's speech echoed the warnings of the drafters of the Bill of Rights that, in the words of Thomas Paine, "those who expect to reap the blessings of freedom must always undergo the fatigue of supporting it."

READING

2 SECRECY AND DEMOCRACY

SECRECY AND DEMOCRACY ARE COMPATIBLE

Mary C. Lawton

Mary C. Lawton presented the following testimony in her capacity as counsel for Intelligence Policy of the Justice Department.

Points to Consider:

1. Please cite examples of openness and confidentiality from our nation's early history.
2. What types of information has Congress singled out as "sensitive"?
3. Why was the press not given advance notice of the Grenada mission?
4. Describe the subject of pre-publication review.

Excerpted from the testimony of Mary C. Lawton before the House Subcommittee on Courts, Civil Liberties, and the Administration of Justice of the House Committee on the Judiciary, September 26, 1984.

Neither our law nor our tradition has condemned secrecy or confidentiality as inherently wrong. Indeed, both have affirmed secrecy in its proper place as essential to our form of government.

I would like to begin with some general observations on the concept of secrecy within an open society. While this might appear to be a paradox it is, in fact, a reflection of the essence of American society which from its inception has contemplated a balancing of values and individual rights.

Openness and Confidentiality

This society has always recognized twin values of openness and confidentiality. The Constitutional Convention that structured our government with its value of openness met in secret. All records of those meetings were sealed for more than 30 years and most of the Framers acknowledged that without secrecy no constitution of this kind could have been developed. The Bill of Rights proposed by our first Congress reinforced the twin goals of openness and confidentiality. While the First Amendment with its guarantee of free press is often cited as the touchstone for openness, it also protects the right to hold certain matters in confidence. The free exercise clause, for example, protects the right to hold private religious beliefs not subject to scrutiny. The right of assembly may, in certain circumstances, include the right to protect the identity of one's associates in confidence.

Neither our law nor our tradition has condemned secrecy or confidentiality as inherently wrong. Indeed, both have affirmed secrecy in its proper place as essential to our form of government. The secrecy of the Grand Jury has always been accepted as protection not only of the individual but of the legal process as well. Our rules of evidence recognize the importance of protecting certain confidential relationships: attorney-client, priest-penitent, physician-patient, and the State secrets privilege which protects both diplomatic and military information which must be held in confidence in the interest of national security.

Sensitive Information

Congress has singled out some types of information as so sensitive that those entrusted with it are subject to criminal penalties if they disclose it. This includes not only the sensitive national security information protected by the espionage and

> ## SECRECY CAN BE A VIRTUE
>
> *The U.S.-Iran-Israel-Nicaragua arms-transfer caper will probably be only a blip on the screen of history unless our fondness for self-flagellation turns it into a serious crisis. The real danger lies not in the misdeeds, but in our overreaction to them.*
>
> *The three U.S. goals in this affair are decent and responsible: to free innocent hostages, to establish contact with moderate elements in Iran, to help freedom fighters in Nicaragua. Most important is helping patriotic Nicaraguans prevent the USSR from extending its evil empire in Central America.*
>
> *Under the circumstances, aspects of our aid to the contras had to be provided under the cloak of secrecy. We democratic Americans don't like secrecy; but in dealing with implacable enemies, covert action is often necessary and right. To be justified, U.S. covert action must be enlisted in a good cause, must employ legitimate and proportional means and, if successful, must advance the cause of genuine peace and security. When these standards are met, secrecy is a virtue.*
>
> Ernest W. Lefever, "When Cause Is Good, Secrecy Is a Virtue," USA Today, December 1, 1986

atomic energy acts but also such diverse information as: cotton statistics, agricultural marketing agreements, census information, certain information filed with the Securities and Exchange Commission, diplomatic codes, civil service examination information, crop information, trade secrets, bank and credit information, tax information, patent information classified for national security reasons, and social security information.

As the wealth of information proliferates, however, and the technology for collecting, storing and transmitting it explodes, it becomes increasingly difficult to strike a proper balance between openness and free communication, on the one hand, and necessary confidentiality on the other. This is reflected in our legal experience over the past decade. In the fall of 1974 Congress enacted privacy legislation instructing the Executive Branch to collect less information, protect it from public disclosure, reduce its sharing among government agencies, and make less use of the social security number as an identifier. . . .

The casual observer might view these legislative "shifts" as "schizophrenic" but on closer scrutiny they merely reflect the twin values of openness and confidentiality and the difficulty in balancing these values in an increasingly complex world.

New Technologies and Solutions

The hearings this subcommittee has undertaken over the past year have focused on just a few of the areas in which the conflict is highlighted. I will comment on each of them briefly.

The press was not given advance notice of the Grenada mission and was not invited along. It protested vigorously and repeatedly cited the fact that it had been accommodated in all previous military actions throughout our history. While the historic argument is important and instructive, it does not address today's circumstance of news reports transmitted by satellite around the world in a matter of seconds. New technologies make new solutions important, particularly when one is dealing with military actions in which the element of surprise is crucial. The Commission which was created following the Grenada action, involved both the press and the military in seeking these new solutions. Only time will tell whether their proposals have arrived at the proper balance. . . .

Criminal Wiretap Provisions

I have already testified before this subcommittee on the subject of the Foreign Intelligence Surveillance Act and the procedures it establishes to strike a balance between national security and individual rights. I do not propose to repeat that here. Rather, I would like to note some of the difficulties that have arisen under the criminal wiretap provisions which were passed in 1968. That law, in my judgment, strikes a proper balance between individual rights and law enforcement needs. It is, however, dated with respect to the new technologies which have developed in the last 15 years. As has been pointed out by previous witnesses, new forms of digital communications, not to mention the capability of miniaturized closed circuit television, have provided new forms of surveillance, some of great importance to law enforcement, which are not encompassed within Title III. . .

The Subject of Pre-Publication Review

Finally, you have requested that I address the subject of pre-publication review. While this concept of reviewing written material of those who are under a non-disclosure obligation in

Illustration by Doug MacGregor. Copyright 1988, *USA Today*. Reprinted with permission.

advance of publication has drawn particular attention since the issuance of NSDD-84, the practice itself is much older and extends beyond the area of national security. Early in my career at the Department of Justice I was assigned the task of reviewing an article prepared by a Department attorney to insure that it did not contain non-public information obtained through his government employment. The regulation prohibiting such disclosure did not then, nor does it now, explicitly require pre-publication review. . . .

Much of the criticism of pre-publication review has focused on it as a form of censorship. I submit that this is a slanted view. As I noted at the outset, Congress has imposed a number of non-disclosure obligations on federal employees enforced by criminal sanctions. It has done so, presumably, because they come into possession of the information under a duty of public trust. Pre-publication review is a protective form of law enforcement to insure that the obligations of public trust are met. It is not the employee's ideas which are subject to review but rather the underlying government information. Of course, one could assert that the criminal sanction, imposed after information is released, is sufficient enforcement. But this overlooks the damage that disclosure may cause to an individual's privacy or economic interests or to the broader interests of the nation.

Reading and Reasoning

WHAT IS EDITORIAL BIAS?

This activity may be used as an individualized study guide for students in libraries and resource centers or as a discussion catalyst in small group and classroom discussions.

   The capacity to recognize an author's point of view is an essential reading skill. The skill to read with insight and understanding involves the ability to detect different kinds of opinions or bias. Sex bias, race bias, ethnocentric bias, political bias, and religious bias are five basic kinds of opinions expressed in editorials and all literature that attempts to persuade. They are briefly defined below.

Five Kinds of Editorial Opinion or Bias

SEX BIAS—The expression of dislike for and/or feeling of superiority over the opposite sex or a particular sexual minority.

RACE BIAS—The expression of dislike for and/or feeling of superiority over a racial group.

ETHNOCENTRIC BIAS—The expression of a belief that one's own group, race, religion, culture, or nation is superior. Ethnocentric persons judge others by their own standards and values.

POLITICAL BIAS—The expression of political opinions and attitudes about domestic or foreign affairs.

RELIGIOUS BIAS—The expression of a religious belief or attitude.

Guidelines

1. From the readings in Chapter One, locate five sentences that provide examples of editorial opinion or bias.

2. Write down each of the above sentences and determine what kind of bias each sentence represents. Is it *sex bias, race bias, ethnocentric bias, political bias, or religious bias?*

3. Make up a one sentence statement that would be an example of each of the following: *sex bias, race bias, ethnocentric bias, political bias, and religious bias.*

4. See if you can locate five sentences that are factual statements from the readings in Chapter One.

CHAPTER 2

TERRORISM, DRUGS, AND THE CIA

3. PROMOTING VIOLENCE: THE DARK SIDE OF U.S. FOREIGN POLICY 25
    John Stockwell

4. PROTECTING DEMOCRACY: SECRECY AND NATIONAL SECURITY IN FOREIGN AFFAIRS 34
    George A. Carver, Jr.

5. THE CIA WAS INVOLVED IN DRUG TRADE 41
    Daniel Siegel and Jenny Yancey

6. NO DRUG SMUGGLING TOOK PLACE 46
    Robert A. Bermingham

7. TERRORISM THREATENS U.S. SECURITY 51
    Richard H. Shultz, Jr.

8. OUR DOUBLE STANDARD ON TERRORISM 57
    Jeff Cohen

READING 3

TERRORISM, DRUGS, AND THE CIA

PROMOTING VIOLENCE: THE DARK SIDE OF U.S. FOREIGN POLICY

John Stockwell

John Stockwell is an ex-Marine and former CIA field case officer. He joined the CIA in 1964 and in his 13 years with the agency, he served in the Congo and Vietnam, and was director of the CIA secret war in Angola. Mr. Stockwell is the highest-ranking CIA officer to go public. This reading is excerpted from a speech Mr. Stockwell delivered at the World Affairs Conference at the University of Colorado, Boulder, April 10, 1987.

Points to Consider:

1. Define the term "destabilization."
2. Who are the contras? How has the United States funded them?
3. Why is propaganda a big part of a destabilization?
4. How and to what extent is the CIA involved in state killing, murder, and torture?

John Stockwell, "The Dark Side of U.S. Foreign Policy," *Zeta Magazine*, February 1989. Reprinted with permission.

Assassination is a part of this program. . . . We can tell you almost to the number how many teachers, health workers, religious workers, elected officials, and government administrators have been singled out and killed in this thing. Terrorism is part of this operation.

What we are here to talk about tonight are grievous problems that face our planet. . . . The CIA—the United States—has a policy of supporting low-intensity conflicts all across the globe. Congressional Oversight Committee staffers tell us the CIA is running a total of 50 covert operations, destabilizing to some degree about one-third of the countries in a world that's already about as unstable as it can get. . . .

CIA Covert Operations

The State Department has been saying all along the purpose is to attack economic targets. This particular action is a technique they call "destabilization." What they mean by destabilization is that you have a government you don't like and it's targeted. It's whimsical; they will attack a country for a few years and then back off sometimes and become friends with that country. We have dramatic examples of that. To put pressure on this government you decide you don't like, you set out methodically to rip apart the social and economic fabric of the country. You set out to create conditions where the farmer can't get his produce to market, where children can't go to school, where women are terrified inside as well as outside their homes, where the hospitals are treating wounded instead of sick people, where government administration simply grinds to a halt and things cease to function and international capital is scared away and the country goes bankrupt.

The Nicaraguan Destabilization

In Nicaragua destabilization began in July 1981 and became a formal program in December 1981, when Mr. Reagan allocated the first $19 million to the CIA to form the contra force. . . .

So we created this force of contras. We recruited them into Honduras. We funded them lavishly. We put uniforms on their backs, boots on their feet, guns in their hands. We gave them training, we gave them medical support, we gave them base camps, we gave them arms, we directed them, we supported them with our planes, we flew weapons and arms in to them, we

> **EXPOSING COVERT ACTIONS**
>
> Stating that United States-sponsored covert operations have jeopardized U.S. national security, threatened the country's democratic system, trampled human rights, denied individual liberties, crippled the administrations of seven U.S. presidents, brought the world to the brink of nuclear war, and resulted in the deaths of more than six million people, a group of former CIA and U.S. military intelligence operatives is out to stop such covert actions. Fifteen former intelligence operatives announced the formation of the Association for Responsible Dissent (ARDIS) at a November 25 news conference in Washington, D.C.
>
> "The founders of this organization have all taken part in covert actions of one sort or another," said retired Marine Col. Philip C. Roettinger, ARDIS president. "We know from personal experience how bad covert actions are. . . ."
>
> "We're distinguished, responsible citizens who are dissenting," said John Stockwell, executive director of ARDIS. Stockwell, a former CIA operations officer who left the agency in 1977 after directing its operations in Angola, has written and lectured widely on "the secret wars of the CIA."
>
> Vicki Kemper, "Ex-U.S. Agents Expose Covert Actions," Sojourners, February 1988, p. 10

supported them with U.S. military. The CIA picked targets from overhead surveillance and told them what to strike and warned them when the Sandinistas were coming. Our navy went up and down the coast protecting them as they raided on the coasts with our navy supervising the mining of harbors to support this operation. Systematically for the last six years, under our direction, these people have been blowing up grainaries, sawmills, bridges, government offices, schools, health centers; they mine roads, they ambush trucks, they raid farms and villages. We have all kinds of documentation of this, if for no other reason than that we have 100,000 of our own citizens down there, taking pictures, writing down the names as people are killed.

Assassinations and Terrorism

Assassination is a part of this program. We've got lists of

names of the people they've assassinated. We can tell you almost to the number how many teachers, health workers, religious workers, elected officials, and government administrators have been singled out and killed in this thing. Terrorism is part of this operation. Now you may have been horrified when the media made a big event out of terrorism in the Mediterranean. They shot an old man in the head and pushed him off the side of a ship and you were horrified; nothing could be more terrible than that, could it? Or when they bomb an airplane or spray an airport with machine guns. But there's lots worse that you can do to people, and the contras are doing it. They go into villages, they haul families out with the children forced to watch, they castrate fathers, peel the skin off their face, put grenades in their mouths and pull the pin, with the children forced to watch them gang-rape their mothers and slash their breasts off. Sometimes for variety they switch it around and make the mothers watch while they slit an 18-month-old baby's throat. Over 5,000 people killed in this thing; this is the figure The *New York Times* uses currently. The figure is obviously greater than that. This is nobody's propaganda. It's been documented and condemned by the World Court, by the Presbyterian Church, by the Methodist Church, by broad segments of the Catholic Church, and once again, by the 100,000 American witnesses who have been down there witnessing, taking photographs. As you know, Mr. Reagan remains unapologetic. He seems to take delight in saying, "I'm a contra." He calls these people the "moral equivalent of [his] founding fathers." And the world gasps at this incredible confession of his family tradition. . . .

Propaganda: Winning People's Minds

Propaganda is a big part of a destabilization. You've got to win people's minds. The propaganda is aimed primarily at the United States and, second, at the world audience. The propaganda against the Sandinistas began under Jimmy Carter, when he authorized the CIA to begin to discredit the Sandinistas. We will never know what the Sandinistas would have done with this country if we'd left them alone to have their way. Maybe they would have turned it into a communist hellhole, who knows? Because we never left them alone to make their own mistakes or do what they would. But what we do know, because we were there standing at their shoulders taking notes, is that they abolished the death sentence. They released 8,000 of these hated guardsmen because they said that they didn't jail anyone unless they had proof of individual

Cartoon by Duffy. © 1989 Des Moines Register and Tribune Company. Reprinted with permission.

crimes. They launched a literacy campaign to teach every Nicaraguan to read and write, something that Somoza, the dictator, who was backed up by the United States, had never gotten around to doing. They set out to build 2,500 clinics so every Nicaraguan would have access to at least some kind of rudimentary medicine. They launched the most serious land reform campaign in the history of Central America, and interestingly enough—remember this when you hear the State Department talking about communism down there—they've kept it a free-enterprise economy. You can go down to Nicaragua and buy a farm or rent an office and put in a telephone and set up a business if you like, and I've known Americans who have done it within the past year. For the first four years they marked the largest economic growth rate in all of Latin America, despite the fact that in the last two of those years we were attacking them to destabilize the economy. They don't have this success anymore because we—the world's richest economy, the world's richest country—have set out to rip apart their economy and we succeeded in dragging them down, to a degree, at least. . . .

Teaching Torture Techniques

For 26 years we had a program in Latin America of teaching torture techniques. . . . The CIA developed a wire that would be powerful enough to carry the current in the hand-cranked generators they were giving these police forces to use that would be fine enough to fit between the teeth, so they could put one of the wires between the teeth and the other one in or around the genitals and crank and submit the victim to the greatest amount of pain, supposedly, that the human body can register.

How do you teach torture? The most famous exponent of this thing was Dan Mitrione. Seven years in Brazil, three years in Uruguay, until he was picked up by the people he was persecuting and assassinated and brought back to the United States. That is about the time this thing was breaking apart, so we know a lot about him and his life and what he was doing.

Now say I'm Dan Mitrione, and you're a class of Brazilian police officers at their academy and I'm teaching you. I give you a lecture, I show you a CIA training film, you read some handouts, but sooner or later you've got to get your hands wet. So Dan Mitrione would have beggars picked up off the streets to be used as guinea pigs in the torture training classes, with the horror being that he knew they didn't know any secrets of any kind to reveal. With the horror being that they couldn't say, "Stop hurting me, here are the names of all my brothers and sisters." All they could do is lie there and scream, and when they would collapse doctors would be brought in to shoot them up with vitamins. When they would eventually die, they would be dumped on the street and their bodies mutilated to strike fear in the people's hearts.

There was a woman in Brazil who was tortured for two years, survived, eventually was released by the international outcry, and testified in international tribunals; you can see her briefly in this film, *On Company Business*. She said that the horror of this thing went beyond the pain itself to the people doing the torture; if they had been raving psychopaths she could have broken mental contact with them. She said they were ordinary, decent people, and that made it harder to break off mentally from them. She told about lying on this table one day, naked in a room full of a half-dozen men who were systematically doing these incredibly painful and degrading things to her body, and there's an interruption. The American is called to the telephone in the next room and the others take a smoke break and she lies there listening to the conversation. And he is saying, "Oh, hi, honey, I guess I can wrap it up here in about an hour or so and pick up the kids and meet you at the Ambassador's on my way home."

The moral in this thing, the reason I dwell on it for a moment, is that we so obviously carefully teach ourselves in our television shows that we're the good guys, that it's Aryan Gestapo maniacs, that it's Slavic KGB monsters. Now the vogue is sadistic Vietnamese colonels in the *Rambo* and *Missing in Action* films that do hideous things to other people. And it's not. It's people who do hideous things to other people. It's red-blooded, American, sane, sober, decent people who do hideous things to other people if their society rationalizes that it's the proper thing to do, as we have done. Dan Mitrione was not a raving psychopath. He was a devout Catholic, a devoted family man, a father of four, and he had devoted his life to torturing and teaching torture even to people he knew were not guilty of anything because his society had said that there was something so noble about the fight against communism that it was a noble thing for him to do. When he was eventually exposed and killed for his activities, he was brought back to the United States and honored with a hero's burial.

Try to count: how many people have we killed with our alter ego, our invisible government activities? There's no record kept; we'll never know exactly, we can only guess. A million people died in Cambodia after we had destabilized it and manipulated it for a decade and a half and then Pol Pot took over and they died in famine and he killed them and then we recognized him as its representative to the United Nations. 800,000 in Indonesia, 75,000 in the Ukraine in 1947; we were involved there too; 20,000 in Hungary in 1956; we were involved there; 20,000 in the Angolan operation that I helped supervise; 5,000+ in Nicaragua today, that's the figure that *The New York Times* gives. Gross millions of people. . . .

Huge Military Burden

We've spent almost 2 trillion on arms to build up our military under Mr. Reagan in the last six years. Militarization of the society, the olive-drab chic, the glorification of war; the conditioning to war in this society begins at the age of two, when the parents put the children in front of the one-eyed babysitter and turn it on. They watch 10 or 15 or 20 episodes of violence every day. . . . It's estimated that young people, when they graduate from high school in this country, have spent more hours watching violence on television than they've spent in the classrooms. . . .

There's more money to be made in war than there is in peace, alas. But profits from military spending are enormous because there is an irrational factor in this. Noam Chomsky makes the point that it's not an irrational system and he's quite right; the people doing it know what they're doing, but we permit it to happen because we're scared, because we allow them to teach us to hate people, to become paranoid, and so we allow them to spend trillions of dollars on arms. The defense corporations make 35 percent profit; that's why they want to make MX missiles. We now have enough missiles in the world to destroy utterly 85 Soviet Unions, to render 20 planets uninhabitable. Mr. Reagan was given a study that showed that we had utter capability of retaliation for this mutually assured destruction with only 300 missiles. But we've got 37,000, the world's got 60,000, and we're in the process of building and deploying 17,000 more. And there is no earthly rationale in terms of making anything safer or defending anybody. What are you going to do, be able to render 21 planets uninhabitable? The reason they want to build and deploy 17,000 more is because there are billions of dollars involved.

What this has done is to create a gigantic burden for that country, a huge military burden. This budget before Congress right now, one third of it is for military spending. To put it another way, the *Washington Post* published a study last year that said that 53 cents of every dollar you pay in taxes goes to the military for hardware, overhead, salaries, and paying off wars in the past. Here we get into the reasons for the destabilizations, the reason they teach us to hate, the reason they take us into petty wars every few years. Simply, the American people would never permit this gigantic military overhead, this burden in our taxes, if the world were truly at peace. They have to have a hostile world, brimming with hostility and violence for us to be sufficiently scared, to see the evidence of the violence, for us to allow them to cut every conceivable social service in this country so they can go on making hundreds of billions of dollars, spending trillions of dollars on defense. And this, I suggest to you, is at least one of the powerful reasons why we have a CIA out there destabilizing every corner of the world.

READING 4

TERRORISM, DRUGS, AND THE CIA

PROTECTING DEMOCRACY: SECRECY AND NATIONAL SECURITY IN FOREIGN AFFAIRS

George A. Carver, Jr.

George A. Carver, Jr., wrote this reading in his capacity as the John M. Olin senior fellow at the Center for Strategic and International Studies in Washington, D.C. He was an intelligence officer for 26 years, special assistant to three directors of Central Intelligence (DCIs), deputy for national intelligence to two DCIs and for three years chairman of the U.S. Intelligence Coordinating Committee in Germany.

Points to Consider:

1. How does the author define "covert action"?
2. What is the author's opinion of the Iran-Contra affair?
3. Why does the author oppose additional restrictions on covert action?

George A. Carver, Jr., "Covert Action an Essential Form of Diplomacy," *Human Events,* December 12, 1987, pp. 1067-1069.

Covert action—despite the risks its employment engenders—is a tool of statecraft no nation should forego, and very few do.

Covert action is a special, often useful and sometimes essential form of secret diplomacy, practiced from time immemorial by all manner of tribes, kingdoms, and nations to further their interests and those of their friends or allies, or to thwart the designs of their adversaries, in situations where it is deemed desirable or necessary to mask the hand of the action in question's true instigator or sponsor.

French and Spanish Help in U.S. Independence

Before we condemn this as invariably sinister, we should remember that we never would have won our war of independence and become a free nation without French and Spanish covert action support, initially handled with great secrecy to keep the donors themselves from becoming openly embroiled in a direct conflict with George III's Britain.

We also should remember that, for similar reasons, private individuals often act in a similar fashion. A benign mother or aunt who tries "to bring two young people together" without being an obvious matchmaker is engaging in covert action, as is anyone who tries to break up an alliance that person considers ill-advised, without getting counterproductively caught in the process.

There are many similarities between covert action and a scalpel. Neither can be wielded successfully by a committee.

Like covert action, a scalpel is useful, even essential in certain situations, though disaster can result quickly if it is not skillfully employed, with a deft and sure hand, by someone who knows what he is doing. Surgeons do not forgo scalpels because if inappropriately or clumsily used they can inflict great injury, even cause death.

Similarly, covert action—despite the risks its employment engenders—is a tool of statecraft no nation should forego, and very few do.

In dealing with the United States, for example, virtually every nation in the world supplements its open diplomacy with various forms of covert action—or unadvertised, unacknowledged lobbying—attempting, with varying degrees of success, to influence our opinions and actions in ways congenial to that nation's perception of its interests. Our adversaries are by no

> **A FACT OF INTERNATIONAL LIFE**
>
> *In most cases, conducting covert action involves contravening, infringing upon, or directly violating the laws of some other nation or nations, with which we are not in a state of war and with which, indeed, we may have treaty relations whose spirit, if not letter, such covert actions may also contravene. (The same is also true of espionage, but that is another matter.) This does not mean we should pass a self-denying ordinance; for covert action is a fact of international life.*
>
> Excerpted from testimony of George A. Carver, Jr. before the House Subcommittee on Legislation of the Permanent Select Committee on Intelligence, March 10, 1988

means the only ones to essay this game; indeed, no one plays it more indefatigably, or successfully, than one of our closest allies—Israel.

To stand any reasonable chance of being successful, a proposed or contemplated covert action must meet several tests.

Conceptually, it should reflect a sense of proportion and perspective. Immediate desires and objectives—such as freeing hostages—never should be allowed to obscure or put at risk larger, long-term national interests, such as punishing and curbing terrorism. It also should be sensible, running with—never against—the grain of local reality in the area in which the operation is to be attempted.

Covert Action by Experts, Not Amateurs

Like surgery, covert action should be conducted by trained, experienced professionals, not entrusted to zealous, well-meaning amateurs with more energy than judgment, whose warheads are better than their guidance systems.

By definition, no covert action should be undertaken unless there is a reasonable chance of keeping it secret, and no such action should be conducted in a way that increases its risk of exposure. Secrecy being hard to maintain under the best of circumstances, however, the political and other costs of exposure should be assessed carefully before a final decision is made to launch any given covert action operation.

Though covert action operations—again, by definition—inevitably involve at least some dissimulation and deception, no such operation should be basically inconsistent or incompatible with any important, publicly proclaimed government policy.

Covert action functions at the margins of policy—ideally, in a quietly supportive way. It can contribute, sometimes significantly, to a policy's success, but it can never be an effective substitute for policy—or for thought. Furthermore, the most brilliantly conceived and skillfully executed covert action operation cannot salvage or redeem a policy that is fundamentally unsound or flawed.

Providing U.S. arms to Iran, by the planeload, in a feckless effort to negotiate the release of American hostages for these already provided arms, failed every test and violated every precept just outlined.

From an American perspective (though not necessarily from an Israeli one), the Iranian exercise was a disastrous fiasco—particularly as a covert action operation.

At its end, Iran's stock of weapons and resultant military capabilities were increased markedly (which may well have been Israel's primary objective), the Reagan Administration and the United States were gravely embarrassed, the sound American policy of not negotiating with terrorists was undercut badly, and the number of American hostages held in or near Lebanon by Shiite militant factions presumably responsive to Iranian influence, such as Hezbollah, had not diminished, but, instead, had increased by half (from six in the summer of 1985 to nine in the summer of 1987).

The Contra-Aid Endeavor

In the process, matters were worsened by grafting the Iran exercise onto the contra support and resupply endeavor (another Israeli suggestion)—thus violating every professional canon of compartmentation and sound security in running covert action operations, with the inevitable result any professional could have predicted. This was doubly unfortunate, since the Contra endeavor was far more sensible and defensible, on its merits, than the Iran quadrille and never should have been tarred with the latter's brush.

As a candidate for election, then re-election, and as President, Ronald Reagan never has made any secret of the fact that he considers the establishment of a Cuban-and Soviet-supported Communist dictatorship in Central America, in Nicaragua, a potential threat to America's vital interests.

Illustration by David Seavey. Copyright 1989, *USA Today*. Reprinted with permission.

Whatever its defects in detailed conception and in execution, the Contra-aid endeavor directly supported—and, unlike the Iran exercise, did not undercut or contravene—well-known, often-enunciated Reagan Administration policy.

In retrospect, it was, nonetheless, clearly not wise or politically astute to handle Contra aid as a covert action operation. Indeed, 20-20 hindsight strongly suggests that the country and Congress, as well as the Administration, would have been far better served if Lt. Col. Oliver North—in open session, with appropriate publicity—had given Congress his forceful presentation of the case for Contra aid in 1982, before the passage of the first of the five "Boland amendments," not at a post-Iran-Contra disaster hearing in 1987.

We cannot go back, however, only forward. We should do so,

furthermore, in the realization that ample mistakes already have been made, at both ends of Pennsylvania Avenue.

Mining these errors for partisan political advantage should not be anyone's primary objective. Instead, the American people and their elected representatives in Washington should focus on protecting our nation's interests, the capabilities—including covert action capabilities—that any administration, of any party, will need to safeguard. . . .

Congressional Assertiveness Over Covert Action

The phenomenon of congressional assertiveness, with an attendant penchant for detailed, legalistic documentation, has been particularly pronounced in the sphere of covert action. . . .

In the present situation, the White House's timorous defensiveness may be as understandable as congressional assertiveness, but both need to be curbed if the national interest is not to suffer.

What is also perhaps not surprising, but certainly regrettable, is that a similar mood seems to have afflicted the White House, where executive orders apparently are being written or revised to impose limitations on covert action that Congress has not yet formally requested or, even less, mandated. . . .

Additional Restrictions Could Be Harmful

In the wake of the Iran-Contra hearings, the concerns and emotions that promoted them, and the additional emotions they engendered, there is a great danger that the covert action capabilities our nation urgently needs—for its security and perhaps even its survival—will be crimped, emasculated, or erased by a new spate of restrictive laws and regulations hastily written in a fit of moralistic pique.

This might suffuse the drafters and enactors of such laws and regulations with a transient glow of self-righteous virtue, but for the country it would be disastrous. If this were to happen, the Iran-Contra committee—whatever its intent may have been—would have done evil that would live longer after that committee was disbanded and its various reports interred in files. . . .

Effective covert action not only needs to be covert by definition, it also needs to be imaginative, flexible and quickly responsive to concrete challenges, problems or situations that cannot be predicted, let alone confided, in advance. The kinds of additional restrictions now being discussed, in the White

House as well as on Capitol Hill, not only would make covert action much more difficult, they easily could make it impossible.

READING
5   TERRORISM, DRUGS, AND THE CIA

THE CIA WAS INVOLVED IN DRUG TRADE

Daniel Siegel and Jenny Yancey

Daniel Siegel co-authored this reading in his capacity as director of public education at the Christic Institute.

Jenny Yancey co-authored this reading in her capacity as southern outreach director at the Christic Institute.

The Christic Institute is a public interest law firm and policy center based in Washington, D.C.

Points to Consider:

1. Who is Ramon Milian-Rodriguez? What role did he play in contra drug dealing?
2. Describe the guns-for-drugs operation. How did it work?
3. What do documents released by the Iran-contra committees of Congress reveal?
4. Why should America's parents be outraged?

Daniel Siegel and Jenny Yancey, "With U.S. Help, Contras Cash in on Drug Trade," *Star Tribune*, March 6, 1988. Reprinted by permission of the *Star Tribune, Newspaper of the Twin Cities.*

The real outrage should come from learning that the Nicaraguan contras and members of the U.S. government are helping drown our society with cocaine.

The Senate recently heard startling testimony of how Panamanian strongman Gen. Manuel Noriega turned his government into a criminal drug and racketeering enterprise. In mid-March, the hearings will resume to focus on another narcotics-backed operation in Central America—this one run by the Nicaraguan contras and their U.S. supporters.

Contra Drug Dealing

Contra drug dealing was discussed at the end of the Panama hearings held by a Senate Foreign Relations subcommittee chaired by Sen. John Kerry, D-Mass. Ramon Milian-Rodriguez, who laundered money for Colombia's Medellin cartel, told the subcommittee that he had given Colombian drug money to the contras through "a liaison with U.S. intelligence."

The "liaison" for the money drops has been identified as Felix Rodriguez, a key player in the contra-resupply operation organized by Lt. Col. Oliver North.

Last year, Milian-Rodriguez told the subcommittee that he arranged the transfer of $10 million of Colombian cocaine profits to the contras between 1982 and 1985. He now says that one of the companies he helped set up to launder the drug cash, Frigorificos de Puntarenas, received a $230,000 State Department contract in 1986 to funnel "humanitarian aid" to the contras.

Guns-for-Drugs Operation

Over the past several years, mounting evidence has implicated the contra network in large-scale drug trafficking. The principal guns-for-drugs operation worked as follows:

Planeloads of Colombian cocaine were flown to farmlands in northern Costa Rica owned by an American rancher named John Hull.

Jose Blandon, Noriega's former adviser, told the Senate subcommittee that Hull worked with the CIA and Gen. Richard Secord's "enterprise," and had received Colombian cocaine on his ranch.

Several sources have told Sen. Kerry's staff that Hull claimed in 1984 and 1985 to be receiving $10,000 a month from the National Security Council.

> **CENSORSHIP BY THE MEDIA**
>
> *A key money-launderer for the Medellin cocaine cartel told Congress in February that he worked with the Central Intelligence Agency, but this information was not reported by the* New York Times, *the* Washington Post, *or the three major networks, even though all covered the hearings.*
>
> *In testimony before the Senate Subcommittee on Narcotics, Terrorism and International Operations, Ramon Milian Rodriguez acknowledged that he laundered more than $3 million for the CIA after his indictment on drug charges in 1983.* New York Times *correspondent Elaine Sciolino failed to mention this in her coverage of Rodriguez's testimony, which was broadcast live on CNN (2-11-88).*
>
> Peter Shinkle, "Media Censor CIA Ties with Medellin Drug Cartel," Extra!, March/April 1988, p. 11

Cocaine on these planes came primarily from Colombia's Medellin cartel, which accounts for about 80 percent of the cocaine smuggled into the United States each year.

The drugs were off-loaded at ranches owned or managed by Hull, and then shipped by air and sea to the United States.

Pilots Confirm Scheme

This operation is confirmed by pilots who participated in the guns-for-drugs scheme. Gary Betzner, one of the pilots, told CBS News about two of his runs to Hull's ranch:

"I took two loads—small aircraft loads—of weapons to John Hull's ranch in Costa Rica, and returned to Florida with approximately 1,000 kilos of cocaine."

Another pilot, Michael Tolliver, in a sworn deposition, told how he flew contra weapons to Honduras and Costa Rica under the direction of veteran CIA operatives Felix Rodriguez and Rafael (Chi Chi) Quintero, and returned to the United States with cocaine and marijuana.

Tolliver said he once returned with over 25,000 pounds of marijuana which he flew directly into Florida's Homestead Air Force Base, where the drugs were unloaded.

Cartoon by Richard Wright. Reprinted with permission.

Revealing Documents

Documents released by the Iran-contra committees of Congress reveal that the Reagan administration has been well aware of contra drug trafficking:

- Oliver North, during an Aug. 9, 1985, meeting with his courier to the contras, Robert Owen, wrote in his notes: "DC-6 which is being used for runs (to supply the contras) out of New Orleans is probably being used for drug runs into U.S."
- A CIA back-channel message to Oliver North from Lewis Tambs, U.S. ambassador to Costa Rica, dated March 28, 1986, has noted on it that contra leader Adolfo Chamorro "is alleged to be involved in drug trafficking."
- A Feb. 10, 1986, memo to North from Owen identifies a DC-4 plane being used by the contras as "used at one time to run drugs, and part of the crew had criminal records. Nice group the Boys (the CIA) choose."

The Real Outrage

Last April, CBS News reported that the CIA directly intervened when the U.S. Customs Service detained indicted drug trafficker Michael Palmer on a flight back from Central America. Customs officials were told to drop the issue of Palmer's extensive drug connections.

In February 1986, Palmer received a $97,000 contract from the State Department's Nicaraguan Humanitarian Aid Office to ship nonlethal aid to the contras.

In March 1986, just before Congress voted for $100 million in contra aid, Ronald Reagan told the nation in a televised speech: "Every American parent will be outraged to learn that top Nicaragua government officials are deeply involved in drug trafficking."

A few days later, the Drug Enforcement Administration said it had no such evidence.

The real outrage for America's parents should come from learning that the Nicaraguan contras and members of the U.S. government are helping drown our society with cocaine.

READING

6   TERRORISM, DRUGS, AND THE CIA

NO DRUG SMUGGLING TOOK PLACE

Robert A. Bermingham

This reading was excerpted from a memorandum that Robert A. Bermingham wrote to House Select Committee Chairman Lee Hamilton and Chief Counsel John W. Nields, Jr. The memorandum appears in the Report of the Congressional Committees Investigating the Iran-Contra Affair. *The report includes findings, conclusions, and recommendations, together with supplemental, minority, and additional views.*

Points to Consider:

1. What people were questioned during the investigation? Was there any evidence of contra drug trafficking?

2. Did the scope of the investigation include determining whether the contras had been independently or individually involved in drug trafficking? Why or why not?

3. Describe the discovery that was made regarding newspaper allegations of contra drug trafficking.

Excerpted from a memorandum to Chairman Lee Hamilton and Chief Counsel John W. Nields, Jr. from Robert A. Bermingham. The memorandum appears as Appendix E in *Report of the Congressional Committees Investigating the Iran-Contra Affair,* 100th Congress, 1st Session. U.S. Government Printing Office, Washington, D.C., 1987, pp. 630-632.

Despite numerous newspaper accounts to the contrary, no evidence was developed indicating that contra leadership or contra organizations were actually involved in drug trafficking.

Overview

Our investigation has not developed any confirmation of media-exploited allegations that U.S. government-condoned drug trafficking by contra leaders or contra organizations or that contra leaders or organizations did in fact take part in such activity. The Select Committee on Narcotics Abuse and the Crime Subcommittee of the Judiciary Committee have been conducting investigation in this area, but, to date, have not developed concrete evidence. The Crime Subcommittee and the Senate Foreign Relations Committee are continuing their inquiries, as is the Special Counsel. It is recommended that after coordination with Chairman Inouye, the Joint Committee issue a statement to the above effect and pledge cooperation with the Senate and House ongoing investigations.

No Evidence of Contra Drug Trafficking

During the course of our investigation, the role of U.S. government officials who supported the contras' and the private resupply effort, as well as the role of private individuals in resupply, were exhaustively examined. Hundreds of persons, including U.S. government employees, contra leaders, representatives of foreign governments, U.S. and foreign law enforcement officials, military personnel, private pilots and crews involved in actual operations were questioned and their files and records examined. Despite numerous newspaper accounts to the contrary, no evidence was developed indicating that contra leadership or contra organizations were actually involved in drug trafficking. Sources of news stories indicating to the contrary were of doubtful accuracy. There was no information developed indicating any U.S. government agency or organization condoned drug trafficking by the contras or anyone else.

The scope of our investigation does not specifically include determining whether the contras have been independently or individually involved in drug trafficking. The Senate Foreign Relations Committee, particularly Senator Kerry; the House Select Committee on Narcotics Abuse and Control under Rep. Rangel; and the Crime Subcommittee under Rep. Hughes of the Judiciary Committee, have been looking into this specific subject

> **SELLING A STORY**
>
> *"This story about drug smuggling and the contras was placed into the ear of Congressional investigators by convicted traffickers,"* said Billy Yout, a special agent in Miami with the Drug Enforcement Administration.
>
> *"These individuals are selling a story to Congress and to the media that they have concocted to have their sentences reduced or to have their cases dismissed,"* he said. *"They had plenty of opportunities to tell their story in court and none of them did."*
>
> Keith Schneider, *"Contra Drug Inquiry Stirs Growing Interest,"* New York Times, *February 24, 1987*

for some time. They have travelled to Central America, interviewed witnesses there and in Miami and have held hearings. Rep. Rangel is quoted in the July 22, 1987 *Washington Post,* as stating his investigation, which started in June of 1986 and includes reams of testimony from hundreds of witnesses, developed no evidence which would show that contra leadership was involved in drug smuggling. His Committee is to give its information to the Crime Subcommittee of the Judiciary Committee which will investigate whether U.S. government officials deliberately ignored drug dealing by individuals who carried supplies to the contras. The Judiciary has engaged a Miami-based investigator.

The Justice Department has issued statements disclaiming any concrete evidence of such activities by U.S. government officials, contra leaders or contra organizations.

Interviews and Investigation

Dave Faulkner, Investigator, Senate Select Committee, advised that the Senate investigation was also substantially negative with regard to contra drug smuggling. On July 21, 1987, Faulkner and the writer conferred with Hayden Gregory, Counsel, of the Crime Subcommittee of the Judiciary. He confirmed that his committee has been and continues to be investigating the question of U.S. government-sponsored contra organizations being involved in drug smuggling. His investigation, including interviews in Central America and Miami of many of the persons named in the newspapers as suspects, has been inconclusive to

Illustration by Craig MacIntosh. Reprinted by permission of *Star Tribune, Newspaper of the Twin Cities*.

date. He confirmed that several of those involved have also been questioned or deposed by the ongoing investigation by Senator Kerry. Gregory confirmed the newspaper account that Representative Rangel's committee is deferring to the Judiciary in this matter. He also stated he has, to date, developed no pertinent information above the level of "street talk."

During the course of our investigation, we examined files of State, Department of Defense, the National Security Council, CIA, Justice, Customs and FBI, especially those reportedly involving newspaper allegations of contra drug trafficking. We have discovered that almost all of these allegations originate from persons indicted or convicted of drug smuggling. Justice has stated that such persons are more and more claiming, as a defense, that they were smuggling for the benefit of the contras in what they believed was a U.S. government-sponsored operation. Typically, they furnish no information which can be confirmed by investigation. In addition to the above-mentioned negative file reviews, interviews with employees of these U.S. agencies have also been negative.

Contra leaders have been interviewed and their bank records examined. They denied any connection with or knowledge of drug trafficking. Examination of contra financial records, private enterprise business records, and income tax returns of several individuals failed to locate any indication of drug trafficking.

It is known that the Special Counsel is looking into this area and that the FBI has pending investigations regarding similar allegations.

Conclusion

It is believed that additional investigation of these allegations is unwarranted in view of the negative results to date, the questionable reliability of the accusers, the fact that two Congressional committees are already deeply involved in such investigations, and that the matter is currently under investigation by the Special Counsel.

READING

7 TERRORISM, DRUGS, AND THE CIA

TERRORISM THREATENS U.S. POLICY

Richard H. Shultz, Jr.

Richard H. Shultz, Jr. wrote this statement in his capacity as an associate professor of international politics at the Fletcher School of Law and Diplomacy and as chairman of the Intelligence Studies Section of the International Studies Association. He is also a member of the secretary of defense's Special Operations Advisory Group.

Points to Consider:

1. Since the 1980s, who has been one of the main targets of terrorist operations?
2. What laid the basis for counterterrorist options against Libya's Colonel Qaddafi?
3. Why does the author suggest covert action as a response to terrorist groups and the radical states that support them?
4. Describe the kind of measures the United States might have to consider in the 1990s.

Reprinted by permission of the publisher, from *Intelligence Requirements for the 1990s*, edited by Roy Godson (Lexington, Mass.: Lexington Books, D.C. Heath & Co., copyright 1989, National Strategy Information Center).

In responding to terrorist groups and radical states that support them, covert action has much to offer because it enables the United States to take offensive or proactive steps.

In the years to come the Soviet Union is likely to pursue new ways in which to insert itself into the Middle East negotiations process. In the past, it has focused on destabilizing the process through assistance to radical Palestinian factions and insurgent movements, as well as by forming alliances with states such as Syria. Recent signs suggest that Gorbachev has initiated a new political stratagem. On the surface, the Soviet Union will seek to create the impression that it is disillusioned with the extremism of those it supported in the past and now wishes to play an active and positive role in the peace process. Covert action and counterintelligence, working in unison, can defend against active measures. This cooperative effort is also appropriate in the Middle East.

Middle East Terrorism

The security and viability of modern Arab regimes in Saudi Arabia, Kuwait, Bahrain, Egypt, Jordan, and Morocco will be a major issue for U.S. foreign policy in the 1990s. These societies have been targeted for destabilization by Iran, Libya, and Syria. From a defensive perspective, there is much the United States can do through intelligence support. Over the years, there have been major successes in this aspect of covert action. A case in point is the long-term provision of assistance and training to the intelligence and security services of King Hassan II of Morocco. There also have been major setbacks, most notably the assassination of Egyptian president Anwar Sadat.

Counterterrorist Covert Operations

The radical regimes seeking to topple moderate Arab states in the region are also involved in supporting terrorist factions. Indeed, for Libya, Iran, and Syria, this is a form of indirect warfare. Available evidence reveals the increasing dimensions and degree to which those carrying out terrorist actions depend on their state patrons. Details now exist about the operational principles, infrastructure, and international and regional coordination of the network that exists among these states and numerous terrorist organizations. Statistics show that during the 1980s terrorist operations have been increasingly directed against U.S. citizens and property. Additionally, there is a rising pattern of lethality, with the bombing of the U.S. embassy and Marine barracks in Lebanon being the most notable examples. Middle East terrorism also has spilled over into Western Europe, where approximately one-third of all terrorist acts are traced back to the Middle East. Here also the United States is one of the main targets.

Against this backdrop, it is necessary for U.S. counterterrorist policy to encompass more than defensive measures. An array of offensive means should be developed and used against terrorist organizations and the states that support their activities. National Security Decision Directive (NSDD) 138 called for an active response against terrorists known to have struck Americans or currently planning such attacks. It likewise laid the basis for counterterrorist options against Libya's Colonel Qaddafi. CIA-directed covert action was viewed as part of a constellation of measures, including diplomacy, propaganda, and economic pressures. All were required if the United States was to establish an effective counterterrorist policy. This included more effective coordination with allies and friends, most importantly in the area of intelligence liaison. However, the transition from the formulation of a counterterrorist policy to its implementation has proven to be exceedingly difficult, especially with respect to the CIA component.

A Human Source Network

The root of the problem in large part lies in the human intelligence base required to support counterterrorist covert operations. To be sure, a great deal of material is available in various open sources on specific terrorist groups. This material needs to be exploited in a more effective way. Intelligence penetration or the cultivation of a source inside a terrorist organization or its support system is equally important. Neither of these are easily achieved. A network of such assets requires a long-term commitment of time and resources. Although this can be supplemented by intelligence provided through liaison arrangements with the intelligence services of states in the region, such measures should not be considered as a substitute for a human source network established by the United States. Such a network has been difficult to establish, however, and not all elements of the U.S. intelligence community are convinced of its value.

Weaknesses and Vulnerabilities

If the United States is to consider employing covert and special operations against terrorist groups and those states that sponsor them, it will require this kind of intelligence base. Once established, collection can focus on the weaknesses and internal vulnerabilities of PLO and Shiite factions. As with any radical movement, these groups are likely to have vulnerability points stemming from ideological divisions and competition among leaders: corruption, factionalism, and weak support services within the organizational infrastructure, and disillusionment among those who carry out operations. These and related weaknesses could serve as the targets for propaganda and political-psychological operations carried out covertly.

The states sponsoring terrorism likewise have weaknesses and vulnerabilities. Substantial evidence has pointed to disaffection within the officer corps of the Libyan military, who often pay the price for Qaddafi's adventurism. Similarly, it appears that disaffection is developing in Iran over the carnage resulting from the war of attrition with Iraq. Likewise, Syria has its own internal vulnerabilities. Propaganda and political action, as part of a broad program and in cooperation with other regional powers, could exploit these and other weaknesses. To do so in the 1990s, the United States will require, in addition to an adequate human intelligence network, the willingness on the part of states such as Egypt, Saudi Arabia, and Morocco to cooperate in these efforts. The latter will not be easily accomplished, given the perception that the United States cannot be counted on to remain involved in such operations and is unable to prevent them from becoming public. This was driven home during the Iran-Contra hearings.

A Broad Program

In addition to propaganda and political action, the United States should consider special military operations for preemptive and preventive strikes against terrorist organizations and for coercive diplomacy against state sponsors. Depending on the nature and size of the operation, these forces might consist of paramilitary elements within the CIA or small units of foreign nationals under CIA control and direction. The operation also might involve special operation forces under the command of the Department of Defense working in liaison with the CIA. In addition to the intelligence base discussed previously, small-scale special military operations require highly sophisticated training of personnel, methods of transportation that permit clandestine infiltration and withdrawal, forward support bases, and the use of deception. Missions currently permitted under the law include harassment, destruction of specific installations, abduction of designated personnel, and the

Cartoon by Richard Wright. Reprinted with permission.

rescue of hostages. The option of special military operations provides for an effective mode to counter, respond to, preempt, and even prevent terrorist attacks. It also can serve as an instrument of coercive diplomacy against those states that persist in aiding and encouraging terrorist organizations. In comparison with conventional capabilities, special military operations are more flexible in that they allow for stealth, surprise, speedy infiltration and withdrawal, and deniability. Many argue that these attributes make this option more attractive than the normal high-profile conventional military response generally adopted by the United States.

To summarize, in responding to terrorist groups and radical states that support them, covert action has much to offer because it enables the United States to take offensive or proactive steps. A note of caution is necessary, however. Isolated propaganda, political action, or special military operations are likely to have little long-term impact. To be effective, they must be part of a broad program of pressures and actions.

Harsher Measures

Thus far, I have focused on those covert operations within existing guidelines that could be employed to disrupt terrorist organizations or coerce and compel those states promoting terrorism and other forms of indirect warfare to desist. In the 1990s, the United States might, out of self-defense, have to consider harsher measures. With respect to hostile states that persist in escalating the use of terrorism and related protracted warfare measures, the issue will be whether to pursue a course of action that, if successful, results in a change of leadership. Additionally, if hard evidence exists, the question is likely to be raised whether lethal measures should be taken against those terrorist leaders who have directed operations resulting in the death of Americans.

Currently, such measures are prohibited under Executive Order 12333. This stipulation was conceived in the aftermath of congressional revelations of prior attempted assassinations. However, are the assassinations of a head of state (for example, Fidel Castro) and the lethal self-defense against terrorist leaders (such as Sheik Mohammed Fadlallah) responsible for the murder of U.S. citizens in comparable circumstances? Both actions are highly controversial and difficult for the United States to entertain, but current positions may be reconsidered if the pattern of events experienced in the past decade continues into the 1990s. The question the United States will have to answer is "If the evidence exists, do democracies have the moral duty to place at risk those responsible for the indiscriminate murder of their citizens?"

READING

8 TERRORISM, DRUGS, AND THE CIA

A DOUBLE STANDARD ON TERRORISM

Jeff Cohen

Jeff Cohen wrote this article for the Los Angeles Times, *in his capacity as executive director of FAIR, a media-watch group.*

Points to Consider:

1. Who is Luis Posada? What is he accused of?
2. Describe what Posada was doing in May 1986.
3. According to the author, what kinds of questions need to be asked?
4. Why have stories about Luis Posada and the CIA's links to right-wing terror groups overseas been under-reported?

Jeff Cohen, "A Double Standard for Those Who Blow Up Passenger Planes," *Star Tribune,* January 10, 1989.

American journalists could begin cutting through the fog by asking George Bush a simple question: If we're serious about punishing terrorists, shouldn't we start with our own?

No sooner was it established that Pan Am Flight 103 had been destroyed by a bomb than the American press went into its predictable ritual. Journalists peppered President Reagan and President-elect George Bush with all the usual questions: How can we bring terrorists to justice? Will we retaliate against any country harboring those responsible for bombing passenger planes?

Tough Talk and Hypocrisy

Reagan and Bush responded with the expected tough-sounding rhetoric. Reagan: "We're going to make every effort we can to find out who was guilty of this savage thing and bring them to justice." Bush pledged to "seek hard and punish firmly, decisively, those who did this, if you can ever find them."

What's wrong with this all-too-familiar script? In a word, hypocrisy.

As many in the media and in the Reagan-Bush administration know, the United States has harbored an accused jet-bombing terrorist. Our government has done nothing to bring him to justice, nor have the media clamored for justice. And there's no doubt, Mr. Bush, about whether "you can ever find him." Folks working for the Reagan administration, in close association with your office as vice president, hired him—long after he was linked to a murderous jet bombing.

Luis Posada and the CIA

The terrorist's name is Luis Posada, a right-wing Cuban exile who worked for the Central Intelligence Agency for years after the Bay of Pigs invasion. Posada says the CIA trained him in the use of explosives. In October 1976, he was the reputed mastermind behind the explosion of a civilian passenger jet that killed all 73 people on board. The Cubana Airlines DC-8 blew up soon after taking off from Barbados en route to Jamaica and Havana.

Posada and other members of the Cuban terror group, Command of United Revolutionary Organizations, were charged in Venezuela with the crime. The two men who admitted planting the bomb identified Posada as a mastermind of the plot.

> **RIGHT-WING TERRORISM**
>
> *The Reagan administration howls about the horrific specter of communist terrorism, singling out leftist groups as the international source of brutal, fanatic terrorism. This assertion is patently false:*
>
> - *In Guatemala, a nation ruled by a right-wing military, 100 people are killed or disappear every month;*
> - *The so-called Contras in Nicaragua routinely torture and murder women, children, the aged, and other "enemies of democracy";*
> - *The nation of Chili—whose military dictator Augusto Pinocet Ugarte enjoys administration support—lives a nightmare of political torture, murder, and mutilation.*
>
> "The Reagan Administration and Terrorism," Utne Reader, August/September 1985, p. 67

But Posada, whose trial was never completed, mysteriously escaped in 1985 from a high-security Venezuelan prison. To this day, he is wanted for terrorism.

Since the Command of United Revolutionary Organizations was led by CIA veterans, the agency learned within days of the jet bombing that Posada and his associates were involved. But the CIA, according to investigative reporter Scott Armstrong, did nothing to bring the men to justice. Bush was then director of the CIA.

Recruited to the Contra Supply Program

After Posada escaped from jail, instead of hunting Posada down, the United States apparently found him a job. Posada was discovered two years ago in El Salvador working as a key overseer in the U.S. operation (Oliver North, William Casey & Co.) to resupply the Nicaraguan contras. In May 1986, a Venezuelan television reporter interviewed Posada from "somewhere in Central America." "I feel good here," Posada exclaimed, "because I am involved once again in a fight against international communism."

Posada was recruited to the contra supply program and was supervised in El Salvador by longtime CIA operative Felix Rodriguez. During this period, Rodriguez reported regularly to

"CONTRA: Endangered Species"

Illustration by Eleanor Mill.

Vice President Bush's office. According to reports from a Senate subcommittee and the *Wall Street Journal*, Posada was one of four leaders of the Command of United Revolutionary Organizations who found work in the contra operation. This despite the fact that the command's members had been involved in bombings and assassination plots, including one in 1976 targeted at Secretary of State Henry Kissinger.

What did the United States do after major American dailies identified Posada as a contra operative in El Salvador? Not much. He was allowed to disappear again.

Questions That Need to Be Asked

Instead of clamoring at Bush for hypothetical responses to still-unidentified terrorists behind the Pan Am explosion, journalists would do better to ask Bush why the United States has protected Posada and friends.

Other questions need asking. If it's terrorism to blow up innocent civilians in the fight against "international Zionism" or "Western satanism," isn't it also terrorism to perform the same acts in the struggle against "international communism"? Or is blowing up civilians acceptable as long as the target is Cuba?

And if it's justified for the United States to retaliate militarily against a foreign country linked to the Pan Am terrorists, would Cuba have had the right to launch an air strike against Washington because of our relations with Posada and his command of United Revolutionary Organizations?

Cutting Through the Fog

The stories of Luis Posada and the CIA's historic links to right-wing terror groups overseas have been under-reported because much of the U.S. media is content presenting a simplistic view of the world where Americans in white hats police the globe of black hats—usually worn by Middle Eastern terrorists.

In some countries of Western Europe and Latin America—where the terrorism issue is analyzed with fewer ideological blinders—people don't automatically see us in white hats. They are as familiar with Luis Posada's U.S. links as we are with Abu Nidal and Libya.

American journalists could begin cutting through the fog by asking George Bush a simple question: If we're serious about punishing terrorists, shouldn't we start with our own?

Reading and Reasoning

RECOGNIZING AUTHOR'S POINT OF VIEW

This activity may be used as an individualized study guide for students in libraries and resource centers or as a discussion catalyst in small group and classroom discussions.

The capacity to recognize an author's point of view is an essential reading skill. Many readers do not make clear distinctions between descriptive articles that relate factual information and articles that express a point of view. Think about the readings in Chapter Two. Are these readings essentially descriptive articles that relate factual information or articles that attempt to persuade through editorial commentary and analysis?

Guidelines

1. Read through the following source descriptions. Choose one of the source descriptions that best describes each reading in Chapter Two.

Source Descriptions
   a. Essentially an article that relates factual information
   b. Essentially an article that expresses editorial points of view
   c. Both of the above
   d. None of the above

2. After careful consideration, pick out one source that you agree with the most. Be prepared to explain the reasons for your choice in a general class discussion.

3. Choose one of the source descriptions above that best describes the other readings in this book.

CHAPTER 3

COVERT ACTION AND FOREIGN AFFAIRS

9. THE CASE AGAINST COVERT ACTION   64
   Clark M. Clifford

10. THE CASE FOR COVERT ACTION   70
    George A. Carver, Jr.

11. THE SECRET CONSPIRACY BEHIND   75
    IRAN/CONTRAGATE
    The Christic Institute

12. NO CONSPIRACY EXISTED   81
    Cliff Kincaid

READING

9   COVERT ACTION AND FOREIGN AFFAIRS

THE CASE AGAINST COVERT ACTION

Clark M. Clifford

Clark M. Clifford served as Secretary of Defense under President Lyndon Johnson. He presented the following testimony before the Subcommittee on Legislation of the Permanent Select Committee on Intelligence.

Points to Consider:

1. What percentage of our government's intelligence activities are covert?
2. How does the author define "covert activities"?
3. Why does the author disagree with the administration's attitude toward the oversight process?
4. Describe the changes Mr. Clifford proposes to improve the oversight process.

Excerpted from the testimony of Clark M. Clifford before the House Subcommittee on Legislation of the Permanent Select Committee on Intelligence, February 24, 1988.

I believe that covert activities have harmed this country more than they have helped us.

Covert activities have become numerous and widespread, practically constituting a routine component of our foreign policy. And with these activities have come repeated instances of embarrassing failure—where the goals of the operations themselves were not fulfilled and unforeseen setbacks occurred instead. I believe that covert activities have harmed this country more than they have helped us. Certainly, efforts to control these activities, to keep them within their intended scope and purpose, have failed.

We have reached the point now where we must reassess the very idea of conducting covert activities. If we are to continue with them and gain any benefit from them, we must find a way to keep them consistent with the principles and institutions of the Constitution and our foreign policy. If we determine that this cannot be done, then I say we are better off without covert activities entirely than with them out of control.

Covert Activities

On this score, we must keep in mind what is meant by covert activities. These are only part, a very small part—perhaps 2 or 3 percent—of the intelligence activities of our government. Covert activities, in my definition, are active efforts to alter political conditions in foreign countries through financial, paramilitary, and other means. That the government should want to disavow responsibility for such activities is understandable.

Over the last year or so, the cost that covert activities can inflict on our system of government also has been clear. Whatever the specific actions of individual responsibility, the sale of arms to Iran and the diversion of profits from those sales to the contras in Nicaragua caused severe damage to our government and the institution of the Presidency. The President's credibility suffered drastically and with it the integrity of the nation's foreign policy.

The Iran-Contra Affair

One of the principal shortcomings of the Iran-Contra affair was the failure of the President to notify the intelligence committees of the government's activities. The oversight process could have served a significant, salutary purpose: giving the President the benefit of the wisdom of those who are not beholden to him, but

> **A THREAT TO AMERICAN DEMOCRACY**
>
> *Even a cursory reading of the Tower commission report provides an all-too-familiar picture of the consequences of permitting the executive branch to conduct covert operations. In both the sale of weapons to Iran and the provision of aid to the contras, the President and his men ignored legal restrictions and lied to the public, to Congress and even to senior officials. They kept information secret to avoid public debate. The result was a disastrous policy and a threat to constitutional government.*
>
> *None of this should have surprised anyone who paid attention to the Senate Intelligence Committee's 1975-76 comprehensive investigation of the Central Intelligence Agency's covert operations. Known by the name of its chair, Senator Frank Church, the committee examined the secret "successes" as well as the public fiascos. It reported on efforts to assassinate foreign leaders, to overthrow democratically elected governments and to spread disinformation. It considered the effects on foreign policy as well as the implications for constitutional government. It also described how the CIA had come home and spied on Americans. The committee concluded that the covert operations had not contributed to the national security but rather had posed a threat to American democracy.*
>
> Morton H. Halperin, *"The Case Against Covert Action,"* The Nation, March 21, 1987

beholden like him directly to the people, and prepared to speak frankly to him based on their wide, varied experience. Had the President taken advantage of notifying Congress, he and the country might well have avoided tremendous embarrassment and loss of credibility.

The Iran-contra affair presents the country with a crucial question: should the laws governing covert activities be changed?

To answer this question, we first might examine the attitude of President Reagan. In his letter to the Senate Intelligence Committee of August 7, 1987, the President said that the current laws are adequate and that any changes could occur by executive order. I strongly disagree.

The Administration's Attitude

In the Iran-Contra affair, the President displayed an attitude that is in direct opposition to the oversight process. You will recall that the President signed a finding that explicitly instructed the Director of the CIA not to notify the Congress of the activity. For ten months, the Director and others involved abided by this instruction. In fact, the President finally notified the Congress only after the activity had become public knowledge. Much later, after the Congress had begun its inquiry, the President in his letter to the Committee supported the concept of notification but insisted on two exceptions. These exceptions would relieve the President of the notification requirement in "cases of extreme emergency" and "exceptional circumstances." I suggest to this Committee that to permit these two exceptions would make any notification requirement meaningless.

Further evidence of the Administration's attitude is the Justice Department's December 1986 memorandum supporting the President's position in delaying notification for ten months. The memorandum offered the novel theory that the President may determine what is timely notice based on the sensitivity of the covert activity. According to this theory, the President would never have to inform Congress of a particularly sensitive activity. This theory clearly would undermine the whole concept of the duty of the President to keep the Congress informed.

The Laws Must Be Changed

Moreover, we find that this continues to be the legal theory of the Justice Department. In testimony before the Senate Intelligence Committee in December 1987, a Department representative made the following statement:

> There may be instances where the President must be able to initiate, direct, and control extremely sensitive national security activities. We believe this presidential authority is protected by the Constitution, and that by purporting to oblige the President under any and all circumstances, *to notify Congress of a covert action within a fixed period of time, S. 1721 infringes on this constitutional prerogative of the President.*

In other words, it is the attitude of the Administration that, whatever laws exist, the President may interpret them as he chooses. This is not the way that I understand our Constitution is supposed to work. So, my answer to the question confronting us today is that the laws governing the oversight process must be changed. And the changes must be specific,

Illustration by John Trever, *Albuquerque Journal.*

direct, and as clear as possible.

I wish to lend my full support to H.R. 3822, the legislation that the Committee is considering today. Late last year, I testified before the Senate Intelligence Committee and supported S. 1721, the companion bill to H.R. 3822. I understand that the committees have worked together on these bills, and I commend your cooperation, as well as its result. The legislation that you have crafted meets the need for change that exists in the important area of notification to the Congress. It would require the President to sign a written finding, setting forth the particulars of a covert activity, normally when approving it but in no event more than 48 hours afterwards. The legislation would require the President to provide the intelligence committees with the signed finding normally before the activity begins but in no event more than 48 hours after it is approved. The President could limit notification to the so-called Group of Eight, but he would have to explain why he was doing so. Findings that purported to validate past activities or authorize illegal measures would violate the law.

Discouraging Further Abuses of Our Foreign Policy

I view these provisions as welcome and worthwhile

improvements in the oversight process; however, I believe that they do not go far enough to redress the recurring perils of covert activities. In order to discourage further abuses of our foreign policy and consequent subversion of our institutions of government, I recommend that the legislation also should contain sanctions to penalize any failure to notify Congress within the required period.

Therefore, I would like to propose for the Committee's consideration a provision to be added to H.R. 3822 that would automatically terminate and prohibit the expenditure of funds for any covert activity with respect to which the President had failed to follow the oversight process. This provision would go beyond the ban on funding of unauthorized activities in the proposed legislation, because it would require the President, within the statutory period, to notify the intelligence committees, as well as sign a finding. Moreover, I would go a step further. According to my proposal, any government officer or employee who knowingly and willfully violated or conspired to violate the prohibition against the expenditure of funds for such a covert activity would face criminal penalties.

This addition to the legislation, in my view and the views of the Constitutional scholars whom I have consulted, would be fully consistent with the letter and spirit of the Constitution. Furthermore, it would be fully warranted by the principle of the rule of law which is our country's creed. . . .

Congress Has an Important Role

I wish to make another point. It bears emphasizing that it was by act of Congress that the CIA was established and exists today; it was by act of Congress that covert activities were authorized and continue to occur. This is so because our constitution confers on Congress the power to make the laws, and the President is charged with taking care that the laws are faithfully executed according to the intent of Congress.

In my judgment, the Constitution clearly provides to Congress an important role in foreign policy, and this role includes the process of overseeing covert activities. It is part of the system of checks and balances among the separate branches of government.

READING

10 COVERT ACTION AND FOREIGN AFFAIRS

THE CASE FOR COVERT ACTION

George A. Carver, Jr.

George A. Carver, Jr., presented the following testimony in his capacity as Olin Senior Fellow at the Center for Strategic and International Studies.

Points to Consider:

1. What is the purpose of covert action?
2. Why does the author believe the President should be able to distance himself or herself from, even disavow, a covert action that he or she approved, even ordered, as chief executive?
3. Does the author believe covert operations are a necessary component of U.S. foreign policy? Why or why not?
4. Explain why the author advises Congress to avoid hasty action.

Excerpted from the testimony of George A. Carver, Jr., before the House Subcommittee on Intelligence, March 10, 1988.

Covert action is a fact of international life. It is something that virtually every nation in the world tries.

What Is Covert Action?

"Covert action" is a term with such a broad scope that it is impossible to define with any degree of precision. It encompasses everything from encouraging a foreign journalist to write a story or editorial which that journalist might well have written anyway to supporting, even guiding, fairly large-scale military activities in foreign lands. Covert action's purpose is to influence the behavior or policies of key foreign areas, in ways that further the interests of the nation mounting the covert action in question, but also in ways that mask that nation's hand and enable its involvement to be denied or, at least, officially disavowed. Perhaps the best way to understand covert action is to think of it as a form of international lobbying that is, ideally, discreet and unadvertised.

The usual euphemism for covert action, employed in the legislation you are considering, is "special activities"—defined in Executive Order 12333 (and elsewhere) as:

> "activities conducted in support of national foreign policy objectives abroad which are planned and executed so that the role of the United States Government is not apparent or acknowledged publicly, and functions in support of such activities. . . ."

As the report of the Iran-Contra Congressional Investigating Committees notes, on page 375,

> "This definition excludes diplomatic activities, the collection and production of intelligence, or related support functions."

Intelligence activities, generally, are not easy for an open, democratic society to conduct effectively, especially in peacetime. For a plethora of reasons, covert action is particularly difficult for a society such as ours, and raises particularly difficult questions—ones that have no universally satisfactory resolutions, let alone any simple answers.

A Fact of International Life

To begin with, there is a consideration that is not polite to acknowledge or discuss, but which has to be faced. In most cases, conducting covert action involves contravening, infringing upon, or directly violating the laws of some other nation or nations, with which we are not in a state of war and with which, indeed, we may have treaty relations whose spirit, if not letter,

> **A VALUABLE INSTRUMENT OF FOREIGN POLICY**
>
> *The whole subject of intelligence activities is a particularly difficult part of the generally troublesome issue of executive-legislative cooperation on the formulation and conduct of U.S. foreign policy. The conflict between the need for consultation and the requirement of secrecy to ensure an effective intelligence system is not easily reconciled. The problem becomes especially acute over the matter of covert action.*
>
> *Covert action, in my opinion, is a valuable instrument of foreign policy, one which is important for the country to have available for certain highly selective situations and circumstances.*
>
> Excerpted from testimony of Brent Scowcroft before the House Subcommittee on Legislation of the Permanent Select Committee on Intelligence, March 10, 1988

such covert actions may also contravene. (The same is also true of espionage, but that is another matter.) This does not mean we should pass a self-denying ordinance, for covert action is a fact of international life. It is something that virtually every nation in the world tries, frequently targeted at us; and some of our closest allies, such as Israel, are among its most indefatigable practitioners. Such considerations do mean, however, that covert action should be used very circumspectly, far more circumspectly than it sometimes has been—as Iran-Contra demonstrates all too clearly. When astutely employed, covert action can be a very useful, effective adjunct to policy, but it can never be a substitute for policy—or for thought.

The President's Role

In this context, there is a salient feature of our political system whose consequences are frequently ignored or brushed aside. Our Constitution combines in one individual, our President, two distinct offices and functions that most other nations divide: the government's chief executive and administrative officer, and the nation's Chief of State. The former is a partisan political figure chosen (in America) by election; the latter, a symbolic focus of national unity supposedly, in that capacity, above the fray of political partisanship. As chief executive officer, a President should certainly be accountable for his and his administration's actions. Nonetheless, it is by no means necessarily in our national interest for our Chief of State to sign "findings" or any other documents directing agencies or officers of the U.S. government to infringe upon or violate the laws of other nations with which we are not in a state of declared war. National Security Council (NSC) staff members, national security advisors, cabinet officers and Directors of Central Intelligence are all expendable; but in our government, Presidents are not. As Chief of State, an American President should be able to distance himself or herself from, even disavow, a covert action that he or she approved, even ordered, as chief executive. This may sound complicated, but so is the real world and, hence, effective diplomacy that runs with the grain of its complex reality.

A Necessary Component of U.S. Foreign Policy

Such messy complexities, and the troublesome issues they raise, lead some to argue that the United States should eschew or abandon covert action altogether. In a perfect world, this might be desirable, but in the world in which we have no choice but to live, it would be folly. One point on which members of the Congressional Committees investigating the Iran-Contra affair were agreed is that, to use their report's words, "Covert operations are a necessary component of our Nation's foreign policy." The real question before Congress, and the American people, is not whether our nation should conduct covert action but, instead, how such operations should be handled, controlled, and reviewed to ensure that they are soundly conceived, efficiently executed and effective, but do not do injury to any of our democratic polity's fundamental interests or basic values.

Congress Must Avoid Hasty Action

Congress was quite understandably distressed by the kinds of covert operations mounted during what we now term "Iran-Contra," by these operations' execution and, particularly, by the way in which Congress was handled with respect to them. No matter how admirable or defensible the Administration's motives and objectives may have been, the way in which these operations were developed and run violated every canon and precept of sound professionalism, not to mention common sense. Furthermore, all other considerations apart, the Administration's manner of dealing with Congress during this episode was both inept and politically tone-deaf.

Congress has ample reason to be irritated at the Administration, and concerned about the way it handled that specific covert action. In dealing with important issues, however, particularly ones as complex as these, all prudent humans — including distinguished members of Congress, and of both of its intelligence oversight committees — should avoid acting hastily, with punitive intent, under the stimulus of irritation.

READING

11 COVERT ACTION AND FOREIGN AFFAIRS

THE SECRET CONSPIRACY BEHIND IRAN/CONTRAGATE

The Christic Institute

The Christic Institute is an interfaith, public interest law firm and policy center. A non-profit organization, the Institute is supported solely by foundations, religious institutions, and private donations. Parallel public education and organizing campaigns complement each legal case, helping citizens press for needed policy changes through the legislative and electoral process.

Points to Consider:

1. What is the Secret Team? Who are some of its members?
2. Describe what happened at La Penca, Nicaragua.
3. Who are Theodore Shakley and Thomas Clines? What Secret Team operations did they take part in?
4. Why did the Secret Team get involved in Central America?

Christic Institute, "The Secret Team Behind Iran/Contragate," 1324 North Capitol Street NW, Washington, D.C. 20002.

The Christic Institute lawsuit, free from the political pressures on the Special Prosecutor and Congressional Select Committees, is pursuing the full truth behind the Iran/Contra scandal including 25 years of criminal activity by the Secret Team.

For the last 25 years a Secret Team of official and retired U.S. military and CIA officials has conducted covert paramilitary operations and "anti-communist" assassination programs throughout the Third World, according to a lengthy affidavit filed in federal court by the Christic Institute.

The international crimes committed by this group in the name of the United States are at the heart of the Iran/Contra scandal. Several Secret Team members, such as retired Maj. Gens. Richard Secord and John Singlaub, and businessman Albert Hakim, are now being investigated by Congressional committees and the Special Prosecutor for their role in the Reagan Administration's illegal arms sales to Iran and the Contras. *For a quarter century this group has trafficked in drugs, assassinated political enemies, stolen from the U.S. government, armed terrorists, and subverted the will of Congress and the public with hundreds of millions of drug dollars at their disposal.*

The La Penca Bombing

The leaders and chief lieutenants of the Secret Team are defendants in a $17 million civil lawsuit filed in May 1986 by the Christic Institute on behalf of U.S. journalists Martha Honey and Tony Avirgan. Plaintiff Avirgan was seriously wounded in the 1984 attempted assassination of Eden Pastora (a dissident contra commander who would not accept the supervision of the largest contra grouping, the FDN) during a press conference at La Penca, Nicaragua, near the Costa Rican border. The attack killed eight, including one U.S. reporter, and seriously injured two dozen.

During their subsequent investigation of the press conference attack, Honey and Avirgan identified the bomber as Amac Galil, an anti-Qhadaffi Libyan sent to the Costa Rican ranch of American John Hull, a CIA operative. The journalists allege that Hull's ranch was used as a transfer point for planeloads of arms destined for the contras and for Colombian cocaine smuggled into the United States. They also found that the same group who planned the Pastora bombing also plotted to assassinate

> ## AN OPERATIONAL ENTITY
>
> *Congress prohibited contra aid for the purpose of overthrowing the Sandinista government in fiscal year 1983, and limited all aid to the contras in fiscal year 1984 to $24 million. Following disclosure in March and April 1984 that the CIA had a role in connection with the mining of the Nicaraguan harbors without adequate notification to Congress, public criticism mounted and the Administration's contra policy lost much of its support within Congress. After further vigorous debate, Congress exercised its Constitutional power over appropriation and cut off all funds for the contras' military and paramilitary operations. The statutory provision cutting off funds, known as the Boland Amendment, was part of a fiscal year 1985 omnibus appropriations bill, and was signed into law by the President on October 12, 1984.*
>
> *Still, the President felt strongly about the contras, and he ordered his staff, in the words of his National Security Adviser, to find a way to keep the contras "body and soul together." Thus began the story of how the staff of a White House advisory body, the National Security Council, became an operational entity that secretly ran the contra assistance effort, and later the Iran initiative. The action officer placed in charge of both operations was Lt. Col. Oliver L. North.*
>
> Excerpted from The Minority Report in Report of the Congressional Committees Investigating the Iran-Contra Affair, *1987*

the U.S. Ambassador to Costa Rica, Lewis Tambs. The assassination would be blamed on the Nicaraguan government in hopes of inciting a U.S. retaliatory strike, while also earning the contra network a $1 million bounty placed on Tamb's head by Colombian druglord Pablo Escobar.

A Criminal Enterprise

Because the La Penca bombing is merely one incident in a long history of criminal enterprise by these defendants, Christic Institute lawyers are prosecuting the suit under a tough anti-organized crime law known as the RICO (Racketeer Influenced and Corrupt Organizations) Act. The 29 defendants include: Hull, Secord, Singlaub, Hakim, Escobar; contra leader Adolfo Calero; businessman Robert Owen; and mercenary

Thomas Posey.

Two important, but relatively unknown, defendants are Theodore Shackley and Thomas Clines, who are both being investigated by the Select Committees. In the affidavit, Christic Institute General Counsel Daniel Sheehan alleges that Shackley and Clines were CIA operatives who supervised covert paramilitary operations against Cuba in the early 1960s. In 1965 the two were transferred to Laos where they provided air support to a druglord named Vang Pao in order to consolidate his control over the opium trade. Some of these heroin profits were used to train paramilitary units of Hmong tribesmen which assassinated over 100,000 suspected "communist sympathizers"—largely non-combatant civilians like town leaders, school teachers, and bookkeepers. Shackley and Cline's associates in this "unconventional warfare" operation included Secord, Singlaub, and a young 2nd Lt. by the name of Oliver North.

Secret Team Operations

In 1971, Shackley and Clines were transferred to the CIA's Western Hemisphere operations, where they directed the "Track II" strategy in Chile that contributed to the 1973 overthrow of Salvador Allende's democratically elected government. The following year, Shackley and Clines directed and financed the Phoenix Project, a political assassination program that killed some 60,000 Vietnamese civilians.

According to the affidavit, Shackley and Clines moved their Secret Team operations into the private sector shortly before the U.S. withdrawal from Vietnam. They subsequently transferred large quantities of Vang Pao drug money to a secret account in Australia and diverted hundreds of tons of military equipment from U.S. arsenals to a secret cache in Thailand.

Following the collapse of the Saigon government, Shackley, Clines, and the Secret Team moved their operations to Iran to help the Shah's secret police identify and assassinate opponents of the regime. It was during this period that Richard Secord, as assistant secretary of defense, and middle-man Albert Hakim, developed the technique of buying U.S. aircraft and weapons from the government at the low *manufacturer's cost,* selling them to Middle Eastern nations at the much higher *replacement cost,* and depositing the profits into secret bank accounts.

Assisting the Contras

The Secret Team next moved to Central America in an attempt

Illustration by Renault, *Sacramento Bee.*

Running mate.

to shore up another tottering dictator—Nicaragua's Anastasio Somoza. When President Carter invoked the Harkin Amendment to cut off further U.S. aid to Somoza, members of the Secret Team stepped in to supply Somoza with arms. After Somoza's overthrow, members of the team armed and advised the dictator's ex-National Guardsmen who were setting up a counterrevolutionary army in Honduras.

This private supply channel continued until the 1980 election of Ronald Reagan, who formally allowed the CIA to mount its own covert paramilitary operation against the Sandinista government. In late 1983, anticipating a congressional cut-off of U.S. aid to the contras, Lt. Col. Oliver North, under the direction of Reagan, Bush, Meese, and Casey, reached out to Shackley, Clines, Secord, and Hakim to re-activate their military supply to the contra operation. This operation was in direct violation of the

Boland Amendment passed by Congress in October 1984 that banned all U.S. officials from providing direct or indirect support for military or paramilitary operations against Nicaragua.

This purposeful violation of the will of Congress and the commission of criminal felonies constitute impeachable offenses by the government officials involved.

When the White House decided in 1985 and 1986 to secretly sell arms to Iran, North recruited the same men to carry out this covert mission. The Secret Team was the critical conduit in the plan to divert profits from the Iran arms sales to the contras.

The Christic Institute lawsuit, free from the political pressures on the special Prosecutor and Congressional Select Committees, is pursuing the full truth behind the Iran/Contra scandal including 25 years of criminal activity by the Secret Team.

READING

12 COVERT ACTION AND FOREIGN AFFAIRS

NO CONSPIRACY EXISTED

Cliff Kincaid

This reading, written by Cliff Kincaid, originally appeared in Human Events, *a national conservative weekly.*

Points to Consider:

1. Who is Daniel Sheehan?
2. Describe the Christic Institute's "Contragate" lawsuit. What claims did they make? Who were the plaintiffs?
3. How did the defendants in the Christic Institute's lawsuit respond to Judge King's decision?
4. Why did Judge King dismiss the Christic Institute's lawsuit?

Cliff Kincaid, "Judge King Flays the Christic Institute," *Human Events,* February 18, 1989, pp. 133-134.

The Christic allegations were based upon nothing more than "unsubstantiated rumor and speculation from unidentified sources with no first-hand knowledge."

The Christic Institute, the radical legal group whose "Contragate" lawsuit was thrown out of court last June for lack of evidence, suffered another serious setback on February 3 when federal Judge James King awarded more than $1 million in attorneys' fees and court costs to the defendants in the case.

Judge King accused the Christic Institute and the plaintiffs of "abuse of the judicial process" by claiming in court that a group of prominent anti-Communists had engaged in a massive criminal conspiracy involving attempted murder and drug trafficking.

"Legal Terrorism"

King found, in effect, that Christic General Counsel Daniel Sheehan had filed a false affidavit in the case. This, of course, is a very serious offense that could possibly lead to his disbarment.

A Harvard-educated former attorney for the American Civil Liberties Union, Sheehan attracted a cult following on the left and raised hundreds of thousands of dollars for the case from Hollywood personalities such as Jane Fonda and Ed Asner and rock stars such as Jackson Browne.

He popularized the notion of a "contra drug connection," a charge that proved damaging to the contra cause, and he was even referred to in a "Cagney and Lacey" dialogue on CBS as a "hero" for his efforts.

However, the television evening news programs have yet to report his recent disgrace in the courts. The two big guns of the liberal press, the *Washington Post* and *New York Times*, mentioned his setback on the inside pages in small stories.

The defendants in the case, who were forced to defend themselves against his "legal terrorism," included Gen. John Singlaub, Maj. Gen. Richard Secord, former CIA official Ted Shackley, Nicaraguan resistance leader Adolfo Calero, Rob Owen, former aide to Lt. Col. Oliver North, and John Hull, an American rancher in Costa Rica who supported North's efforts.

These men had one thing in common: they had participated in military and covert operations against the Communists.

> **HYSTERICAL CONCLUSIONS**
>
> *President Reagan and his staff made mistakes in the Iran-Contra affair. It is important at the outset, however, to note that the President himself has already taken the hard step of acknowledging his mistakes and reacting precisely to correct what went wrong. He has directed the National Security Council staff not to engage in covert operations. He has changed the procedures for notifying Congress when an intelligence activity does take place. Finally, he has installed people with seasoned judgment to be White House Chief of Staff, National Security Adviser, and Director of Central Intelligence.*
>
> *The bottom line, however, is that the mistakes of the Iran-Contra affair were just that—mistakes in judgment, and nothing more. There was no constitutional crisis, no systematic disrespect for "the rule of law," no grand conspiracy, and no Administration-wide dishonesty or coverup. In fact, the evidence will not support any of the more hysterical conclusions the Committees' Report tries to reach.*
>
> Excerpted from The Minority Report in Report of the Congressional Committees Investigating the Iran-Contra Affair, 1987

A "Secret Team"

The case dates back to May 1986, when the Christic Institute, with the backing of liberal church groups, filed suit under the Racketeering Influenced and Corrupt Organizations act (RICO), a law designed to put the Mafia out of business. The suit claimed the defendants were linked to a "secret team" that had tried to assassinate Nicaraguan resistance leader Eden Pastora and had been running other criminal operations financed by the sale of drugs and arms.

The plaintiffs were "journalists" Tony Avirgan and his wife, Martha Honey, who were activists against the Vietnam War. Avirgan visited Hanoi during the war and wrote about it in an article entitled, "From Hanoi with Love."

Avirgan, now a stringer for CBS News and other media in Central America, was slightly injured when a bomb exploded at a 1984 Pastora news conference in La Penca, Nicaragua.

Combating "Venomous Radical Leftists"

After more than two years of fighting the suit, defendants Singlaub and Owen told *Human Events* that Judge King's award of attorneys' fees and court costs was a "moral victory."

Shackley said, "The decision underscores the fact that the suit has always been a political case without merit. It was never a legitimate civil suit. It was an attempt to set a political agenda by abusing the legal system."

Secord said his reaction was one of "considerable gratification." He added, "It is a very welcome development in combating these venomous radical leftists."

However, Tom Spencer, attorney for Singlaub, cautioned that it is too early to celebrate. He said the likelihood of collecting the money is like "me seeing the man in the moon."

Curious Legal Maneuvering

He told *Human Events* that it is still unclear whether the Institute, in addition to the plaintiffs, is liable for the award. And, even if it is, he said, the Institute might try to avoid payment by declaring bankruptcy and re-emerging under a different name. "They might call it the Sheehan Institute," he said.

In throwing out the suit last June, Judge King said the Christics had presented no evidence tying the defendants to the Pastora bombing.

In awarding attorneys' fees and court costs, Judge King said, the Christic Institute attorneys "must have known prior to suing that they had no competent evidence to substantiate the theories alleged in their complaint."

Describing Christic General Counsel Daniel Sheehan's curious legal maneuverings, the judge noted that Sheehan had supplemented the legal complaint with an affidavit "outlining the purported testimony of 79 witnesses who Mr. Sheehan stated had factual knowledge that these defendants set and exploded the bomb that caused plaintiffs' injuries."

"The 79 witnesses were identified only by number," he said, and Sheehan "refused to identify the names and addresses of the vast majority of the 79 witnesses until ordered to do so by the court."

However, Sheehan then appealed this order, a process that "prevented the defendants from taking depositions of these witnesses and delayed orderly discovery for many months," King said.

Daniel Ortega

Illustration by H. Payne. Reprinted by permission of UFS, Inc.

"After all the appeals were exhausted and plaintiffs complied with the order to reveal the names of their witnesses," he added, "the reason for the plaintiffs' adamant refusal became apparent."

Failure to Produce Admissible Evidence

"Specifically, the names and identities of 20 of the 79 witnesses were totally unknown to Mr. Sheehan or the plaintiffs."

Judge King said, "Several of the disclosed witnesses later stated under oath that they did not know Mr. Sheehan, had never spoken to him, or flatly denied the statements he had attributed to them in his affidavit. The remaining witnesses did not furnish any statements that would be admissible. Much of the testimony of these witnesses involved conversations they allegedly had with other people, which is the hearsay testimony inadmissible at a trial."

The plaintiffs were permitted to conduct two years of discovery, the judge noted, but "failed to produce any admissible evidence" against the defendants. The Christic allegations were based upon nothing more than "unsubstantiated rumor and speculation from unidentified sources with no first-hand knowledge."

===== Reading and Reasoning

INTERPRETING EDITORIAL CARTOONS

This activity may be used as an individualized study guide for students in libraries and resource centers or as a discussion catalyst in small group and classroom discussions.

Although cartoons are usually humorous, the main intent of most political cartoonists is not to entertain. Cartoons express serious social comment about important issues. Using graphics and visual arts, the cartoonist expresses opinions and attitudes. By employing an entertaining and often light-hearted visual format, cartoonists may have as much or more impact on national and world issues as editorial and syndicated columnists.

Points to Consider:

1. Examine the cartoon in this activity. (See next page.)
2. How would you describe the message of this cartoon? Try to describe the message in one to three sentences.
3. Do you agree with the message expressed in this cartoon? Why or why not?

Illustration by Dan Hubig. Reprinted with permission of Pacific News Service.

CHAPTER 4

DOMESTIC SPYING AND POLITICAL DISSENT

13. THE FBI'S CRIMINAL BEHAVIOR   90
    Mike Zielinski

14. THE FBI WAS RIGHT ABOUT CISPES   97
    Human Events

15. SPYING ON THE CHURCHES: 102
    THE POINT
    Garrett Brown

16. SPYING ON THE CHURCHES: 108
    THE COUNTERPOINT
    James P. Turner

17. TARGETING THE SOCIALIST   112
    WORKERS PARTY
    Political Rights Defense Fund

18. THE CASE AGAINST THE SOCIALIST   118
    WORKERS PARTY
    Gary B. McDaniel

READING

13 DOMESTIC SPYING AND POLITICAL DISSENT

THE FBI'S CRIMINAL BEHAVIOR

Mike Zielinski

Mike Zielinski wrote this article as a special report for The Guardian, *an independent radical newsweekly.*

Points to Consider:

1. How was the FBI forced to divulge the details of its domestic surveillance?
2. What did FBI Director William Sessions' testimony reveal?
3. Who is Michael Ratner? Describe his reaction to the FBI's conclusions.
4. Why did the FBI decide to investigate CISPES?

Mike Zielinski, "FBI Whitewash on Domestic Spying," *The Guardian,* September 28, 1988, pp. 1, 6.

"The mentality behind the CISPES investigation was the same mentality that produced the FBI's excesses of the 1960s."

Does the spirit of J. Edgar Hoover live on at the FBI? Not according to the self-serving testimony of FBI Director William Sessions during congressional hearings on the bureau's five-year investigation of opponents of U.S. policy in El Salvador.

A Clean Bill of Health

Following a self-examination, the FBI gave itself a clean bill of health at public hearings convened by the Senate Select Intelligence Committee and the House Subcommittee on Civil and Constitutional Rights on Sept. 14 and 16. The bureau denied that its domestic spying operation, directed at the Committee in Solidarity with the People of El Salvador (CISPES) and scores of other groups working to end U.S. intervention in Central America, was politically motivated or that the bureau engaged in systematic violations of constitutional rights.

But the FBI's finding that its CISPES probe was not politically motivated flies in the face of massive evidence to the contrary. During the course of a far-flung investigation government agents photographed people attending demonstrations, employed paid informers to infiltrate meetings, ran police checks on the license plates of cars parked outside CISPES offices, and studied anti-intervention publications and leaflets in order to identify critics of U.S. policy.

Campaign of Harassment and Surveillance

The FBI cast a wide net in its search for "subversion." The government's campaign of harassment and surveillance eventually mushroomed into 178 "spinoff" investigations, as the bureau's files bulged with references to groups ranging from the United Auto Workers and Southern Christian Leadership Conference to SANE and the American Friends Service Committee.

The FBI's intensive surveillance of Central America organizations ultimately involved 52 of the bureau's 58 field offices. FBI officials stated that the investigation cost a minimum of $800,000 and involved the equivalent of 10 agents working full-time for two years. A lawsuit by the Center for Constitutional Rights (CCR) forced the FBI to divulge the details of its domestic surveillance in early 1988. According to CCR's David Lerner, "Quite clearly the mentality behind the CISPES

> ## AN OUTRAGEOUS DISCOVERY
>
> *I was outraged to learn the FBI had been spying on First Run Features. My company is one of the largest in the business of selling and renting social/political issue films to universities, libraries and religious, labor, women's, veterans' and community organizations. Our films have won hundreds of awards from educators, libraries, film festivals, even Academy Awards. . . .*
>
> *My outrage over being spied on is not diminished by learning we weren't the primary target of the probe. The potential chilling effect on uninhibited dissemination of ideas is just as real. People have a right to learn about Central America from as many sources as possible, not just the official government version and not even just from the three TV networks.*
>
> *We deal in films, not bombs; that may explain why the FBI is suspicious of us. The fact the FBI is watching companies like mine, and not criminals, might explain our high crime rate.*
>
> Seymour Wishman, "This Kind of Probe Is Outrageous Waste," USA Today, February 4, 1988

investigation was the same mentality that produced the FBI's excesses of the 1960s."

"An Administrative Mess-Up"

Sessions, however, contends the bureau was a victim of "managerial or supervisory inadequacies." The FBI director told the hearing, "I have seen no evidence whatsoever that the conduct in question was either illegal or motivated by any improper purpose.". . .

The FBI's report was gratefully received by a majority of the congressional committee members, many of whom praised the bureau's "honesty" and "refreshing candor." Among the exceptions was Rep. John Conyers (D-Mich.). Conyers challenged the internal report, summing up its conclusions as a case of "a few bad apples in this bunch, but . . . no systemic problem." In confronting Sessions, Conyers explained that "I would have felt much better . . . if you'd come back and told us that this was something more than an administrative mess-up, because that lets everyone off the hook."

A Vicious Campaign of Intimidation

Sessions recommended that future surveillance operations be accompanied by training for all FBI personnel on how to deal with political activity protected by the First Amendment, prompting Senator Howard Metzenbaum (D-Ohio) to declare, "It flabbergasts me that at this point in the FBI's history you're just getting into the issue of training in First Amendment rights."

Metzenbaum also called into question FBI assertions that no constitutional rights were violated in the course of its domestic spying. He cited the example of an Ohio professor investigated by the bureau for inviting a member of a CISPES affiliate to address his class and for including a question on U.S. policy in El Salvador on a final exam. The FBI's Cincinnati office initially denied that the professor was a subject of investigation, a claim Metzenbaum labeled an "outright falsehood," based on a reading of the bureau's internal records.

Immediately following the Senate hearing, CCR attorney Michael Ratner blasted the FBI's conclusions. Ratner characterized the agency's internal report as "cosmetic action . . . . Political spying was part and parcel of the FBI's work and wasn't just a little mismanagement problem." Ratner added that "to suspend agents for 14 days for what was clearly a massive invasion of the constitutional rights of Americans is, I think, outrageous."

The scale of the FBI investigation belies the bureau's contention that only low-level agents were responsible and that the surveillance was not politically motivated. FBI files contain numerous derogatory references to CISPES's politics, while the New Orleans office sent a memo to national headquarters stating that "it is imperative at this time to formulate some plan of attack against CISPES." According to CISPES executive director Angela Sanbrano, "The Reagan administration had to resort to a vicious campaign of intimidation because of the effective work the anti-intervention movement has done in organizing public opposition to the U.S. war in El Salvador and throughout Central America."

Link to Salvador's Government

In absolving itself of illegal spying the FBI sought to scapegoat Frank Varelli, a Salvadoran paid by the bureau to infiltrate and inform on the Dallas chapter of CISPES. The FBI contends its initial investigation of CISPES was spurred on by Varelli's claims

Illustration by David Seavey. Copyright 1988, *USA Today*. Reprinted with permission.

that the solidarity group was a threat to U.S. national security. The FBI has since acknowledged that CISPES's campaigns—which include organizing demonstrations, public education and raising funds for El Salvador's popular movement—are legitimate political activities protected by the Constitution.

Varelli used information from a series of articles by Salvadoran death squad leader Roberto D'Aubuisson which appeared in a right-wing Mexican magazine. In addition, the FBI relied on material from the John Birch Society and the Liberty Lobby, an anti-Semitic group with links to ex-Nazis and the George Bush presidential campaign. Varelli, currently suing the FBI for back wages, maintains he told his superiors what they wanted to hear.

Evidence of a close connection between the FBI and the Salvadoran National Guard was left largely unexplored during the hearings. Varelli contends the bureau worked closely with Salvadoran security forces, providing the National Guard with the names and flight numbers of Salvadorans being deported from the U.S. to El Salvador. Historically, the guard has played a particularly brutal role within the Salvadoran military; its members have been implicated in the assassination of Archbishop Romero and the rape and murder of four U.S. churchwomen in 1980. Varelli also claims the FBI paid an employee at the Salvadoran consulate in Los Angeles to pass along the names of U.S. citizens applying for visas to travel to El Salvador.

Spying Continues

When questioned by Rep. Don Edwards (D-Calif.) about information-sharing between the FBI and the Salvadoran military, Sessions conceded that "it's possible," while denying that any bureau official other than Varelli was involved. However, CCR has uncovered FBI memoranda predating Varelli's employment which document bureau discussions with the National Guard. An FBI teletype from 1981 calls for papers confiscated from a refugee facing deportation to "be furnished to the captain of Taca [El Salvador's state-owned airline] for passage to El Salvador, National Guard. . . ."

Freedom of Information Act requests filed by CCR have turned up evidence that the FBI continues its spying on the Central America anti-intervention movement. Despite bureau assurances that the CISPES probe was shut down in 1985, documents obtained from the Chicago FBI office reveal ongoing surveillance of public demonstrations through an investigation labeled "Nicaragua Terrorist Matters."

The FBI still maintains open investigations under a variety of pretexts, including "Nicaragua Proposed Demonstrations" and "Salvador Leftist Activities in the U.S."

CISPES and CCR are demanding an immediate end to harassment and surveillance of groups working for peace with justice in Central America and that the FBI expunge from its records the names of all individuals and organizations who were illegally investigated. The FBI has indicated it will maintain its files unless contacted by individuals who wish to have their names removed. Sessions says these requests will be dealt with on a case-by-case basis. CCR, on behalf of CISPES, is considering a lawsuit to force the bureau to honor a Freedom of Information Act request for access to the CISPES files, while demanding that the government purge its permanent files of all information obtained through the FBI's spying operation.

READING

14 DOMESTIC SPYING AND POLITICAL DISSENT

THE FBI WAS RIGHT ABOUT CISPES

Human Events

This reading originally appeared as an article in Human Events, *a national conservative weekly.*

Points to Consider:

1. Why did the FBI decide to investigate CISPES?
2. Describe the Farabundo Marti de Liberacion Nacional (FMLN).
3. How did CISPES get started?
4. What other groups did the FBI investigate during the same period as the CISPES investigation?

"Why FBI Was Right on CISPES," *Human Events,* February 13, 1988, pp. 144-145.

CISPES wants to portray itself as being the victim of the FBI because of its opposition to the Administration regarding Central America.

Although extreme leftist groups are trying to portray it otherwise, FBI Director William Sessions last week emphatically denied that the bureau had carried out a "massive surveillance" effort aimed at intimidating "foes" of the Administration's Central American policy. . . .

CISPES and the FMLN

Members of CISPES and their extreme-left allies may now be feigning shocked innocence over being the targets of FBI "harassment" merely because they disagreed with Administration policy. But the real reason for the probe, as Sessions made clear, were allegations that CISPES was actively involved in providing support for the terrorist Farabundo Marti de Liberacion Nacional (FMLN).

A teletype sent out from FBI headquarters told operatives "this investigation is not concerned with the exercise of rights guaranteed by the United States Constitution, but rather, with the involvement of individuals in the CISPES organization in international terrorism as it affects the El Salvadoran government, and the collection of foreign intelligence and counterintelligence information as it relates to the international terrorism aspects of this investigation."

The *New York Times*, in its coverage of Sessions' press conference, styled the FMLN as a "leftist rebel group that has acknowledged its involvement in several violent attacks against the American-backed government in El Salvador."

But why not the "democratically elected government of El Salvador"? The government, after all, held elections open to all groups, and the Communists were soundly rejected.

And why not, as Sessions did, call the FMLN what it really is, "a foreign terrorist organization"? Even the *Times* admitted that the organization took responsibility for the 1983 murder of Lieutenant Commander Albert Schaufelberger, an American military attache stationed in El Salvador.

A Communist Terrorist Organization

The FMLN is, in fact, a communist terrorist organization dedicated to the revolutionary and violent overthrow of the government in El Salvador. The group maintains close ties to

> ## INVESTIGATING CRIMINAL BEHAVIOR
>
> *Most Americans sleep better knowing the lights are on around the clock at the FBI's J. Edgar Hoover headquarters building. But apparently some don't, including those who are howling the loudest about the FBI's investigation of the leftist Committee in Solidarity with the People of El Salvador (CISPES).*
>
> *In this case, G-men followed a trail of illegal support for a Central American terrorist operation right into the USA's network of lesser-known leftist groups, including CISPES. Please note, the FBI was investigating criminal behavior, not political views. The individuals involved in the CISPES inquiry were reportedly suspected of criminal activities ranging from harboring illegal aliens to gun-running and sedition.*
>
> *The FBI has long tracked unsavory characters within the myriad of extremist political operations of the left and the right. Of course, this requires an occasional look at the entire forest as well as the individual trees. Apparently in the CISPES case, the FBI concluded these political radicals were not officially or organizationally supporting illegal activities.*
>
> *Those who come close to the line of legal/illegal activities in their zealous pursuit of political extremism shouldn't be surprised when official eyebrows are raised in suspicion. After all, it's the FBI's job to discern between those who may be naively duped and those who readily embrace violence as a means to an end.*
>
> Peter B. Gemma, "FBI Has Done Nothing to Violate Our Trust," USA Today, February 4, 1988

and receives aid from Moscow, Havana, and Managua. It has received endorsement from Yasir Arafat and the PLO.

According to Sessions, "the terrorist activities of the FMLN included bombings, kidnappings, assaults, and assassinations." The FMLN was responsible for terrorist attacks against civilians attempting to vote in El Salvador's 1982 Constituent Assembly election, an election in which the FMLN was invited to participate. In 1985, the FMLN staged an attack on a cafe in the capital city of San Salvador, killing 13, among them four unarmed U.S. Marines and two private U.S. citizens. In that same year, the Communist guerrillas kidnapped the daughter of El Salvador's president, Jose Duarte.

It is to the support of this organization that CISPES is committed. In fact, CISPES is a front of the FMLN.

What Is CISPES?

CISPES grew out of a 1980 trip to America by Farid Handal. Handal's brother, Sharik, is general secretary of the Communist party in El Salvador and has served as a member of the FMLN's general command. While Farid was in the U.S. drumming up support for a pro-FMLN group, Sharik was visiting the USSR and various East Bloc countries to obtain military and financial aid.

With extensive help and cooperation from the Communist Party, U.S.A., and the Cuban delegation to the United Nations, Farid's efforts resulted in the creation of CISPES. CISPES now serves as the main U.S. front for the FMLN and its political arm, the Democratic Revolutionary Front (FDR).

CISPES has committed itself to ending any U.S. presence in Central America, and has called for material support to the FMLN guerrillas. According to a report by Michael Waller and Allan Brownfeld, CISPES in 1983 "raised over $450,000 in cash, food, and clothing for the FMLN's 'liberated zones,' working through fronts called 'People to People Aid,' and 'Medical Aid to El Salvador.'". . .

Other FBI Investigations

In fact, while CISPES wants to portray itself as being the victim of the FBI because of its opposition to the Administration regarding Central America, during the same period CISPES was being investigated, 1983-1985, under William Webster's tenure as director, the FBI also looked into the operations of groups that actually support Administration policy.

"Since 1982, the FBI has conducted several Neutrality Act investigations involving groups operating inside the United States which were allegedly involved in illegally furnishing funds, weapons and other support to what are traditionally identified as right-wing organizations," Sessions told reporters.

Among these groups, the *Washington Times* reports sources in the Justice Department as citing, were the U.S. Council for World Freedom, a pro-contra fund-raising and support group headed by Major General (Ret.) John Singlaub and the National Defense Council which, under the leadership of former Army Captain Andy Messing, Jr., has delivered food, clothing, and medical supplies to the contras.

Is the FBI Out of Control?

CISPES and the CCR have been joined by the *New York Times*, the *Washington Post* and Democratic members of Congress, including Senate Select Committee on Intelligence members Bill Bradley (N.J.) and David Boren (Okla.) and Rep. Don Edwards (Calif), who chairs the House subcommittee that oversees FBI operations, in raising the specter of an FBI out of control because of this investigation.

But there is absolutely no evidence that the FBI directed its field agents to engage in any illegal activities.

The FBI, in fact, closed down its CISPES investigation in June 1985 after the Justice Department concluded "it appeared that CISPES was involved in political activities involving First Amendment rights and not international terrorism."

READING

15 DOMESTIC SPYING AND POLITICAL DISSENT

SPYING ON THE CHURCHES: THE POINT

Garrett Brown

Garrett Brown presented the following testimony in his capacity as associate director of the New Institute of CentroAmerica, a language school and cultural exchange program located in the city of Esteli, Nicaragua.

Points to Consider:

1. What characteristics distinguish the OCBC break-ins from common burglaries?
2. Describe the timing of the break-ins.
3. Who does the author believe is responsible for the break-ins? Why?
4. Do you agree with the author's conclusions? Why or why not?

Excerpted from the testimony of Garrett Brown before the House Subcommittee on Civil and Constitutional Rights of the House Committee on the Judiciary, February 19, 1987.

The government would clearly gain by being able to disrupt the work of our organizations and by creating an atmosphere of distrust and fear within those organizations.

My name is Garrett Brown. I am the Associate Director of the New Institute of CentroAmerica (NICA), which is a language school and cultural exchange program located in the city of Esteli, Nicaragua. Our U.S. offices are housed in the Old Cambridge Baptist Church in Cambridge, Massachusetts. Between October 1984 and September 1986 I worked in the Cambridge office and have been working in Esteli for the last five months. . . .

In addition to NICA, I am also speaking on behalf of the members and sanctuary committee of the Old Cambridge Baptist Church (known as OCBC) and the Central America-related organizations also housed in the church, including the Central America Solidarity Association (CASA) and the New England Central America Network (NECAN).

I am here today to talk about the series of burglaries that the Church and our organizations have been subjected to over the last two years. OCBC has been broken into eight times since offering sanctuary to a Salvadoran woman trade unionist in October 1984. Some 29 offices have been affected by these intrusions.

The OCBC Break-Ins

As in break-ins at other sanctuary churches around the country, the OCBC break-ins have not had the character of common burglaries to obtain money or valuables. Items of value, including cash, credit cards, cameras and office equipment, have been left behind while organizational files, membership lists, financial records, desk drawers, and cabinets have been examined. On several occasions, mail was opened and rifled. On other occasions, phone answering machines and cassettes containing outgoing information and incoming calls were taken.

The timing of break-ins has been closely linked to public events related to Central America. Most break-ins have occurred at times when the Reagan Administration's Central America policy was either being debated before Congress in Washington or being protested in peaceful, legal demonstrations and educational activities in the Boston area and around the

> ## SPYING ON "PEACE BISHOPS"
>
> *The Federal Bureau of Investigation (FBI) admitted that it has been keeping files on two prominent U.S. Catholic "peace bishops."*
>
> *The FBI stated in a February 2nd letter, "Reference is made to your pending Freedom of Information Privacy Acts requests pertaining to (Detroit Auxiliary Bishop) Thomas Gumbleton and (Seattle Archbishop) Raymond Hunthausen. Documents pertaining to your request have been located; however, before release can be made, they must be reviewed to ascertain if they warrant classification under current standards."*
>
> *The FBI's letter was a response to this newspaper's Freedom of Information Act (FOI) requests, filed in September 1986 (with the approval of the bishops concerned), that sought to establish whether the FBI was spying on Catholic bishops who have spoken out against the U.S. nuclear arms buildup. The* National Catholic Reporter *is awaiting replies to other FOI requests on other bishops and Catholic organizations.*
>
> Jim McManus, "FBI Admits It Has Files on U.S. 'Peace Bishops'," National Catholic Reporter, February 20, 1987

country.

For example, NICA's office was burglarized on April 20, 1985, the very day more than 50,000 people, including the NICA staff, marched in Washington protesting U.S. policies in Central America. In the March 1986 break-ins, a note denouncing CASA's efforts to aid "Indian-Hispanics" was left behind in the ransacked office which was the organizing center of "Central America Week" activities in Boston. Phone answering machines with "hotline" information about more than 35 scheduled activities were stolen.

Moreover, the Church was broken into immediately before, immediately after, and on the first anniversary of the December 1984 arrival of the Salvadoran refugee being given sanctuary at OCBC.

A Political Motivation and Character

These facts all indicate the break-ins have a political motivation and character, rather than being examples of petty crime. In our opinion, these break-ins are politically motivated reprisals against a sanctuary church designed to disrupt our organizations' work opposing the U.S. government's war policies in Central America, to harass and intimidate our members and supporters, to create an atmosphere of fear and an air of illegitimacy, and to undermine the Church's financial ability to offer low-cost rent to peace and social justice organizations. . . .

In thinking about who would undertake such politically-motivated efforts, one has to ask two questions: "Who has done this kind of thing before? And who would benefit by it?" In our opinion, one comes up with the same answer to both questions: The United States government.

Government Agencies Responsible for Break-Ins

As we now know from Congressional investigations and individual lawsuits during the 1970s, the FBI, INS, Alcohol, Tobacco and Firearms Division of the U.S. Treasury Department, among other government agencies, have engaged in systematic disruption and harassment campaigns against peaceful, legal organizations. These operations have included widespread break-ins of the character which have hit our offices. The post-Watergate restrictions on these types of activities were all lifted in the early days of the Reagan Administration, and various government agencies, such as the INS, have already admitted to similar operations in recent years.

Moreover, the FBI has already acknowledged that it is maintaining active files on the Church and the organizations housed within it. The Bureau has refused to say why or how these files are being maintained.

We learned through Congressional and courtroom testimony in the 1970s that government agencies sometimes directly organized the break-ins, sometimes indirectly sponsored "civilian" organizations and individuals to conduct these operations, and sometimes simply "allowed" previously planned activities by "civilians" to occur. In all cases, however, government agencies bear the responsibility for these activities.

This is the historic record of who has done these kinds of things before.

The Government Has a Clear Motive

The U.S. government is also the prime suspect of who would benefit from a disrupted, intimidated peace movement. As has been demonstrated in numerous polls, the government's policies

Cartoon by Horsey. Reprinted with special permission of King Features Syndicate, Inc.

in Central America are extremely unpopular with the American public. They are the most unpopular with those who know the most about what U.S. policy actually is and what its actual impact in the region is.

The government would clearly gain by being able to disrupt the work of our organizations and by creating an atmosphere of distrust and fear within those organizations. Were they successful in undermining our effectiveness in disseminating information about U.S. policy to the public, and in organizing the overwhelming majority opposition to that policy, it would be an important advance for the government towards implementing those policies.

Given the Administration's determination to press forward with its Central America war policies in the face of overwhelming domestic and international opposition, the government has a clear motive in attempting to weaken the effectiveness, influence, and impact of our organizations. . . .

Conclusion

In conclusion I would like to say that I don't think it is coincidental that those of us who are for peace in Central America are working peacefully, legally, and in the light of day; while those who are for continued war in Central America are working violently, illegally, and in the dark of night.

The U.S. government's entire policy in Central America, as is now becoming all the more apparent in the current Congressional and media "Iran/Contragate" investigations, is based on violence, illegal acts, lies, and deceptions. It is only logical that this policy would have a domestic impact of exactly the same character.

The Administration has tried and is desperately trying to keep the American public from knowing the true nature and impact of its policy in Central America. Attacks on those of us trying to get out that information, and then efforts to deny that these attacks even exist, fit naturally into a policy of secret arms deals, Swiss bank accounts, drug trafficking, and covert action.

READING

16 DOMESTIC SPYING AND POLITICAL DISSENT

SPYING ON THE CHURCHES: THE COUNTERPOINT

James P. Turner

James P. Turner presented the following testimony in his capacity as deputy assistant attorney general for the Civil Rights Division of the Department of Justice.

Points to Consider:

1. Why did the committee chairman contact the Director of the FBI?
2. What kind of federal criminal civil rights statutes must be considered before the FBI can begin an investigation?
3. When asked to check for evidence of a pattern linking the burglaries, what did the FBI discover?
4. Were federal or local governments involved in the break-ins? Please explain your answer.

Excerpted from the testimony of James P. Turner before the House Subcommittee on Civil and Constitutional Rights of the House Committee on the Judiciary, February 20, 1987.

There has been no evidence developed to support the bare allegation of federal or local government involvement in any of the break-ins.

I am appearing today to describe the response of the Department of Justice with respect to the allegations of a series of break-ins occurring at churches and offices of organizations opposed to the federal government's policies in Central America.

The Request for an Investigation

In January of 1986, the chairman of this committee first wrote to the Director of the FBI suggesting that the Bureau consider investigating this series of burglaries on the theory that there may be foreign agents responsible. After consultation with the relevant department components, the Director advised the chairman on April 11, 1986, that there did not appear to be an investigative predicate on these matters. Last December the chairman and Congressman Feighan wrote to the Attorney General asking that the matter be reconsidered and forwarded new information regarding a burglary of the International Center for Development Policy (ICDP) that had occurred in November 1986. After evaluation of this information the Civil Rights Division requested the FBI to conduct an investigation of the ICDP burglary, which investigation is presently being completed.

The Department's ability to investigate alleged criminal conduct is confined to the particular offenses which are prohibited by the federal criminal code. Although I am in a position only to comment directly on those offenses for which the Civil Rights Division has enforcement responsibility, I am advised there is at this time no basis for the application of other federal criminal laws to the conduct in question. With that understanding, I am pleased to relate to the subcommittee the process by which we determined to request the present investigation.

Federal Criminal Civil Rights Statutes

The federal criminal civil rights statute which we most frequently utilize to bring prosecutions requires some evidence of official or law enforcement wrongdoing before there is sufficient predicate to investigate.

Other federal criminal civil rights statutes require some evidence of interference by conspiracy, or by force or threat of force, with a federally protected right, as defined by statute or court opinions, before an investigation may be requested. One such right is the right to petition Congress for redress of

> *To date, insufficient information has been obtained suggesting any prosecutable violation of federal law — either civil rights law or other statutes — regarding the burglaries of "Sanctuary" churches or other organizations that have been identified to us. We are, however, continuing to assess the situation and should such information be provided appropriate investigation will be conducted.*

grievances. This is so because the right to petition the federal government for redress of grievances has been held by the Supreme Court to be a right inherent in national citizenship. As such it is protected against conspiratorial interference from any source, whether public or private. The Division has traditionally declined to ask the FBI to investigate incidents that are local in nature based upon a mere perception or suspicion that some federal law may be implicated.

Our initial decision to investigate then is determined by the existence of some credible evidence either of official involvement in the wrongdoing at issue or of evidence of a conspiracy to interfere with the right to petition the federal government.

No Evidence Exists

The FBI initially was asked to check for evidence of a pattern linking the burglaries brought to our attention and, to date, no such evidence has been developed. Local police had responded in each instance and their reports make clear that many of the reported burglaries have involved no more than thefts for monetary gain. Police in Boston, for example, have arrested three common criminals for church burglaries — one thief was even arrested in the act.

There also has been no evidence developed to support the bare allegation of federal or local government involvement in any of the break-ins.

Insufficient Information Has Been Obtained

However, the information provided to the Department by you and others regarding ICDP described it as an organization primarily engaged in lobbying and working with Congress. Therefore, the facts suggested a possible basis for federal jurisdiction and, accordingly, an investigation was requested. In

Illustration by H. Payne. Reprinted by permission of UFS, Inc.

addition, we are presently evaluating information obtained about multiple break-ins at the Old Cambridge Baptist Church in Cambridge, Massachusetts, to determine whether further information is required to exercise federal jurisdiction.

We evaluate each incident on the basis of the information that is available. To date, except to the extent specified, insufficient information has been obtained suggesting any prosecutable violation of federal law—either civil rights law or other statutes—regarding the burglaries of "Sanctuary" churches or other organizations that have been identified to us. We are, however, continuing to assess the situation and should such information be provided appropriate investigation will be conducted.

READING 17

DOMESTIC SPYING AND POLITICAL DISSENT

TARGETING THE SOCIALIST WORKERS PARTY

The Political Rights Defense Fund

This reading was excerpted from a public letter by the Political Rights Defense Fund (PRDF). PRDF was established in 1973 to publicize, raise funds, and win support for the Socialist Workers Party lawsuit.

Points to Consider:

1. What were the main gains won through the SWP lawsuit against the FBI and other government agencies?

2. Why did the Justice Department drop its appeal?

3. Now that the Political Rights Defense Fund has accomplished its goal, what is it doing?

Excerpted from a public letter by the Political Rights Defense Fund, Box 761, Church St. Station, New York, New York 10007.

We have accomplished a lot—a historic victory for political rights. . . . "Everyone who wants to fight can fight in better shape today, and rights for all were expanded."

On March 17 the Department of Justice filed notice with the U.S. Court of Appeals dropping its appeal seeking to overturn an historic ruling on behalf of political rights issued by federal Judge Thomas P. Griesa. Judge Griesa had ruled on behalf of the suit filed in 1973 by the Socialist Workers Party (SWP) and Young Socialist Alliance (YSA) against FBI spying and disruption. . . .

Main Gains That Were Won

Concretely, the main gains won through the SWP lawsuit against the FBI and other government agencies were:

● We forced out the broadest picture of government covert domestic crimes ever revealed.

In his decision Judge Griesa provided an extensive summary of Washington's illegal operation, going back to 1938, the year the SWP was founded. He chronicled the FBI's use of 1,300 undercover informers who were paid $1,680,592 for spying on, disrupting, and stealing 12,600 documents from the SWP and YSA from 1960 to 1976. He detailed 57 disruption operations conducted by the FBI, including poison-pen letters, malicious articles planted in the press, instances of harassment and victimization, attempts to get SWP members fired from their jobs, and efforts to disrupt collaboration between the SWP and civil rights and anti-Vietnam war groups.

He enumerated 208 "black bag jobs" and 20,000 wire-tap days and 12,000 bug days of electronic surveillance of the offices and homes of the SWP and its members, resulting in the theft and photographing of 9,864 private documents.

Forcing out these facts has educated millions about the unconstitutional political police character of the FBI, CIA, Immigration and Naturalization Service, Secret Service, and other government agencies that were defendants in the case.

● For the first time ever a federal judge ruled that government informers are not "neutral observers," but disruptive spies whose conduct violated the right to privacy and the freedom of association of those targeted.

● Also for the first time, Judge Griesa ruled that FBI burglaries

> **A UNIQUE DECISION**
>
> *A 36-year FBI effort to disrupt the Socialist Workers Party through wiretapping, bugging, "black-bag jobs," anonymous letters and harassment was illegal and "patently unconstitutional," U.S. District Court Judge Thomas Griesa ruled. . . .*
>
> *Leonard Boudin, a constitutional lawyer and attorney for the Socialist Workers Party, a small Trotskyite offshoot of the Communist League, called the decision "unique. It is the first judicial decision on what the FBI did during this terrible period. Never before has a court examined in depth, made a case study of decades of intrusion by the FBI into the political affairs of an organization."*
>
> *FBI and Justice Department spokesmen declined comment on the 210-page opinion.*
>
> Margot Hornblower, *"Socialists Win Damages,"* The Washington Post, August 26, 1986

are violations of the Fourth Amendment, which was written to protect the people against illegal searches by the government.

• Judge Griesa ruled that surreptitious disruption operations such as that conducted against the two socialist groups are against the law. He strengthened his ruling by awarding the SWP and YSA $264,000 for damage caused by the FBI's informers, burglars, and disrupters.

• Judge Griesa ruled that the rights and protections of the U.S. Constitution apply to open advocates of social revolution such as the SWP, thus strengthening these rights for everyone.

Extensive Investigation Conducted

To make this determination, the judge conducted an extensive investigation into the revolutionary views and political activities of the two socialist groups. He concluded that after 40 years of intensive spying "there is no evidence that any FBI informant ever reported an instance of planned or actual espionage, violence, [or] terrorism." Therefore, the FBI's conduct was "wholly incompatible with the SWP's First Amendment right to freely assemble and freely speak on political matters."

• The judge's ruling made no distinction between those SWP and YSA members and supporters who are citizens and those who are not. All, regardless of where they were born, are protected from being victimized for their political views and activities. This ruling is an important new expansion of the right of immigrants to be politically active in the United States.

• The judge held that appeals—even by the president—to "national security" could not be used to justify the illegal operations conducted against the SWP and YSA, writing that "the FBI exceeded any reasonable definition of its mandate and had no discretion to do so." Even the highest official of the executive branch of the government is subject to the rule of law, Judge Griesa stressed.

• Finally, the judge issued a permanent injunction barring government agencies from using any information in the 10 million files gathered illegally by the FBI to target and victimize people today. . . .

All together, these advances are a significant gain for the rights of all who want to be politically active, to defend their union from attack, or who support constitutional rights. The decision of the Justice Department to drop the appeal means that Judge Griesa's ruling stands as the final judgment in the case.

Why Did the Justice Department Drop Its Appeal?

The SWP had a strong case against the government's political police. And it was prosecuted well by lead attorney Leonard Boudin and the broader team of able attorneys. But these were not the decisive reasons that the Justice Department was forced to throw in the towel and drop its appeal. . . .

Most recently, revelations have documented a nationwide covert drive by the FBI to "break" the Committee in Solidarity with the People of El Salvador (CISPES). As a result of the efforts of CISPES and the Center for Constitutional Rights, the FBI has been forced to admit that between 1981 and 1985 it spied, harassed, and collected over 3,700 pages of files on hundreds of individuals, unions, and organizations that oppose U.S. policy in Central America.

These revelations have exploded government claims that the FBI had been "cleaned up" since the SWP filed its lawsuit in 1973 and no longer targets people solely because of their political views and associations.

For these reasons, the government was in a weakened position to conduct a major fight to overturn Judge Griesa's rulings. To have done so would have required rehearsing the facts of their decades-long operation against the SWP and YSA before the

'Do you have the feeling we're being watched?'

Illustration by Edd Uluschak, *Edmonton Journal*.

public, which they were unwilling to do in the context of the spreading belief that it is the government, not political activists, who are the subversives.

The most telling sign of the government's weakened position was its stubborn refusal to answer reporters' questions about why the Justice Department dropped the appeal. . . .

PRDF's Goal Accomplished, Office Closed

We can now close out the accounts and shut down the office. Over the last fifteen years we have raised and expended more than $1.4 million to help cover the legal, publicity, and office expenses of the fight around the SWP case. Additional hundreds of thousands in legal fees were met with contributions from the Bill of Rights Foundation. The Socialist Workers Party has contributed its entire damage award of $264,000 to help meet as many of the outstanding debts and obligations taken on by the defense fund as possible.

We have accomplished a lot—a historic victory for political rights. In a press conference held in chief counsel Leonard Boudin's office to announce the government's decision to drop its appeal, SWP National Secretary Jack Barnes concluded:

"We can say that our victory helps *encourage* people to engage in political activity, *increases* the space for politics, *expands* the de facto use of the Bill of Rights, *increases* the confidence of working people that you can be political and hold the deepest convictions against the government and it's your right to do so and act upon them, and *weakens* their ability to prepare secretly for war and repression. Everyone who wants to fight can fight in better shape today, and rights for all were expanded."

READING

18   DOMESTIC SPYING AND POLITICAL DISSENT

THE CASE AGAINST THE SOCIALIST WORKERS PARTY

Gary B. McDaniel

This reading is excerpted from the affidavit of Gary B. McDaniel. The affidavit was submitted to Judge Thomas Griesa as part of an offensive by the Justice Department against the judge's ruling that he will bar the government from any use of illegally obtained spy files on the Socialist Workers Party and Young Socialist Alliance.

Points to Consider:

1. What service does the Office of Federal Investigations (OFI) provide?

2. Describe Executive Order 10450 and the Atomic Energy Act of 1954.

3. Why does the U.S. Office of Personnel Management need access to information regarding the Socialist Workers Party or the Young Socialist Alliance?

4. What would happen if the OFI were denied access to this information?

"Government Agencies Challenge Ruling Against FBI Spying," The Political Rights Defense Fund, May 1987.

Mere membership in the Socialist Workers Party (SWP) or the Young Socialist Alliance (YSA) would not, in and of itself, be an issue. . . . OFI considers this information important because these organizations in the past were opposed to our form of government and the national interest.

I am the Chief of the Investigations Operations Division, Office of Federal Investigations (OFI), U.S. Office of Personnel Management (OPM). In that position, I have oversight responsibility for the performance of the personnel background investigations done nationwide by OPM, including the assembly and transmittal of the final product to the customer agency.

The Office of Federal Investigations

OPM's OFI conducts approximately 250,000 background checks or investigations each year on individuals who are applicants for or holders of positions in the United States government or government contractors. Approximately 150,000 of these are on individuals who will have access to sensitive classified information, materials, or sites. All of these latter investigations are done under authority of Executive Order 10450 (E.O. 10450) and the Atomic Energy Act of 1954. Both the Order and the Act require that persons who will be granted such access be, among other things, loyal to the United States and its democratic system of government.

OPM does not itself grant security access clearances (except to its own employees) but, rather, conducts a variety of background investigations on a reimbursable basis as a service to almost all Executive branch departments and agencies except for the Department of Defense and some other investigative agencies. These customer agencies grant or deny security clearances based largely on the reports of investigation furnished by OPM. To provide an adequate investigation upon which such critical decisions can be made, OPM must have access to as much information as possible. This is necessary to present a complete picture of each individual investigated as to his suitability, reliability, and loyalty. Among OFI's sources of information are the various investigative and intelligence agencies of the United States, including the Federal Bureau of Investigation (FBI).

> ## SECURITY SIGNIFICANCE
>
> ***Executive Order 10450, section 8(a)(5), provides that***
>
> > *Membership in, or affiliation or sympathetic association with, any foreign or domestic organization, association, movement, group or combination of persons which is totalitarian, Fascist, Communist, or subversive or which has adopted, or shows a policy of advocating or approving the commission of acts of force or violence to deny other persons their rights under the Constitution of the United States, or which seeks to alter the form of government of the United States by unconstitutional means*
>
> ***is of security significance.***
>
> In the course of conducting Personnel Security Investigations the Defense Investigative Service (DIS) routinely requests that the Federal Bureau of Investigation (FBI) review its files for information pertaining to the subject of our investigations. These records checks may, among other things, disclose that the subject of a DIS investigation has been affiliated with an organization characterized by Executive Order 10450.
>
> The information obtained from the FBI may serve to corroborate or establish an affiliation with such an organization. However, the membership in such an organization, per se, is not the security concern. Rather the establishment of this affiliation provides a basis for expanding the investigation.
>
> Excerpted from the affidavit of Thomas J. O'Brien, director of the Defense Investigative Service, Department of Defense

Making Security Determinations

Mere membership in the Socialist Workers Party (SWP) or the Young Socialist Alliance (YSA) would not, in and of itself, be an issue under E.O. 10450 or be the final determinant in the granting or denying of a security clearance. The information is, however, a lead that OPM must fully address and resolve through its investigation. Such factors as the extent of involvement, the recency of it, whether such involvement was with full knowledge of the intents and aims of the organization and, if the person is no longer a member, the nature and extent of the person's activities since being a member, all must be considered when making a security clearance adjudication. Consequently, OPM's investigation cannot consist only of a fact of membership but must delve into all these other aspects to present as complete and accurate a report as is possible. Access to the information thus permits OPM to conduct the investigation in such a manner to assure that all relevant facts, including favorable or mitigating information, are included in the report and are considered by the agency making the security determination.

Either OFI or the customer agency which receives OFI's report of investigation does a subject interview in almost all cases. During this interview, individuals being investigated are made aware of the information developed and afforded the opportunity to explain, refute, or make a statement regarding the information. All such responses are made a part of the investigative file. In addition, OPM's investigative files are rigorously safeguarded from unwarranted disclosure, and the subjects of OFI investigatory records have the protection of the Privacy Act and the Freedom of Information Act.

Programs Could Be Seriously Compromised

If OFI were denied access to, or could not use, information on membership in the SWP or the YSA obtained by the Federal Bureau of Investigation between July 1, 1955, and September 1976, either now in OFI files or gained in the future from FBI name checks, the OFI investigation and the customer agencies' security programs could be seriously compromised. OFI considers this information important because these organizations in the past were opposed to our form of government and the national interest. A person who successfully conceals such membership or activities and seeks security access for purposes harmful to the national interests or security could gain such access and be in a position to do extreme damage to the United States. The access in question could include classified defense information and nuclear weapons materials and sites.

Any information obtained from the FBI through a name check request, including information on SWP or YSA membership, becomes part of the file on the particular individual involved. All files are maintained, either as hard copy or on microfilm, in secure, locked storage with access limited only to authorized personnel. Release of these files is governed by and in accordance with established security procedures and law. Since the information in question is maintained by individual file, it is not accessible by subject matter. Any effort to retrieve

President Eisenhower's attorney general, Herbert Brownell, testifying at 1981 trial of Socialist Workers Party suit.
Illustration by Diane Jacobs.

information specifically concerning the SWP or YSA could only be done by retrieving and reviewing each and every one of the over four and one-half million files currently in the system. No files are maintained concerning the SWP or YSA per se.

Reading and Reasoning

EXAMINING COUNTERPOINTS

This activity may be used as an individualized study guide for students in libraries and resource centers or as a discussion catalyst in small group and classroom discussions.

The Point

It is the government's responsibility to ensure national security. When members of radical political groups pose a threat to the nation's well-being, then the government is justified in monitoring the activities of these groups.

The Counterpoint

The government has no right to conduct unwarranted surveillance of radical political groups. Although it must preserve national security, the government is violating the First Amendment rights of the groups it chooses to spy on.

Guidelines

Part A

Examine the counterpoints above and then consider the following questions.

1. Do you agree more with the point or counterpoint? Why?
2. Which reading in this book best illustrates the point?
3. Which reading best illustrates the counterpoint?
4. Do any cartoons in this book illustrate the meaning of the point or counterpoint arguments? Which ones and why?

Part B

Social issues are usually complex, but often problems become over-simplified in political debates and discussions. Usually a polarized version of social conflict does not adequately represent the diversity of views that surround social conflicts. Examine the counterpoints. Then write down possible interpretations of the issue other than the two arguments stated in the counterpoints.

CHAPTER 5

COVERT ACTION AND INTELLIGENCE: IDEAS IN CONFLICT

19. MASSIVE CIVIL LIBERTIES VIOLATIONS 126
    Herman Schwartz

20. PRESENT LAWS PROTECT LIBERTY 133
    William H. Webster

21. FORSAKING DEMOCRACY: 138
    THE COLD WAR AND COVERT ACTION
    Eric Black

22. PROTECTING DEMOCRACY: 146
    INTELLIGENCE AND COVERT ACTIONS IN
    HISTORY
    The Minority Report of the Iran-Contra Affair

READING

19 COVERT ACTION AND INTELLIGENCE

MASSIVE CIVIL LIBERTIES VIOLATIONS

Herman Schwartz

Herman Schwartz presented the following testimony in his capacity as professor of law at American University.

Points to Consider:

1. Why did the FBI install wiretaps and bugs on Dr. Martin Luther King, Jr.? Who knew that the FBI was doing this?
2. Describe Operation CHAOS.
3. Has wiretapping and bugging of Americans served any useful purpose? Please be specific in your answer.
4. Why is intelligence surveillance difficult to control?

Excerpted from the testimony of Herman Schwartz before the House Subcommittee on Courts, Civil Liberties, and the Administration of Justice of the House Committee on the Judiciary, January 24, 1984.

It really doesn't make much difference who is in power. Once in office Jefferson, Lincoln, Wilson, Roosevelt, Truman, Eisenhower, Kennedy, and Johnson all committed grave violations of civil liberties when they felt threatened.

Where national security is concerned, privacy and confidentiality have rarely carried much weight. The CIA has opened hundreds of thousands of letters and screened millions more; the National Security Agency has intercepted millions of cables and international phone calls; the FBI, the military, the CIA, the IRS, and others have listened in on millions of phone calls in the United States involving countless numbers of people; the FBI, IRS, and others have perpetrated hundreds and perhaps thousands of burglaries; informants and *agents provocateurs* have been introduced into peaceful groups, often with tragic results for family, friendships, jobs, and health. All of this has been ostensibly for the purpose of obtaining intelligence to protect our national security against domestic and foreign threats, but all too often solely to stifle dissent. . . .

Encouraging Use of Bugs and Taps

The Church Committee Report and discovery proceeding in court, especially in the on-going *Socialist Workers Party* case, have now provided detailed confirmation of suspicions that national security taps and bugs have been used primarily for political and other illegal purposes. Virtually every intelligence agency, and many other government agencies as well, have violated the law again and again. Virtually every President since Franklin D. Roosevelt has approved, condoned, and often encouraged such violations. Attorneys General either ignored or encouraged. Congress deliberately chose not to know. Official lawlessness has been commonplace.

In 1941, Attorney General Francis Biddle approved a wiretap on the Los Angeles Chamber of Commerce as "persons suspected of subversive activities." Four years later, a high official in the Truman Administration and a former aide to Roosevelt were both tapped.

In the early 1960s Attorney General Robert Kennedy authorized, in the name of national security, an investigation of the sugar lobby, and approved taps on ten telephone lines of a law firm, three taps on executive branch officials, two on a Congressional aide, and a microphone in the hotel room of

> **THE PRIVATE GOVERNMENT**
>
> *"This private government within the White House is the President's personal responsibility. If the CIA mines the harbors of Nicaragua and the U.S. refuses to explain this to the World Court, that can be done only with a wink and a nod from the President. . .For years now, the CIA and the National Security Council have been skirting the law, trying to achieve by covert action what they cannot justify or explain to Congress."*
>
> —James Reston,
> New York Times
>
> The Washington Spectator, *January 15, 1987*

Harold D. Cooley, the Chairman of the House Agriculture Committee. The result, according to the Church committee, was "a great deal of politically useful information."

The FBI and Dr. Martin Luther King

At the 1964 Democratic Convention, the FBI installed wiretaps and bugs on Dr. Martin Luther King, Jr., the Student Nonviolent Coordinating Committee, and on other civil rights organizations, and transmitted a great deal of information to President Johnson's aides about the Mississippi Freedom Democratic party's challenge to the regular Mississippi delegation.

In an effort to destroy Dr. King, J. Edgar Hoover had the FBI install 16 taps and eight room bugs in Dr. King's hotel rooms and offices from the Fall of 1963 until his assassination in 1968; New York and Miami police also bugged Dr. King at the FBI's instigation, even in church. This produced thousands of hours of tapes, from which the FBI tried to disseminate allegedly damaging material to *Newsweek*, the *Los Angeles Times*, and other media. Tapes were also sent to Dr. King and to Mrs. King, in what he and his aids considered an effort to drive him to suicide. The Church Committee concluded that "there is no question that officials in the White House and Justice Department, including President Johnson and Attorney General Katzenbach, knew that the Bureau was taking steps to discredit Dr. King."

"A Wealth of Information"

President Nixon authorized taps on four journalists and 13 government employees, allegedly to ascertain the source of leaks on foreign affairs matters. The tap on one of these, Morton Halperin, was in effect 21 months, revealed no information relevant to leaks, was not based on any reasonable suspicion of him, was in contravention of internal Justice Department procedures, and was maintained for almost two years despite repeated reports soon after installation that it was producing nothing of value. The taps were also on White House staffers who had no contact with national security matters. Although producing no evidence as to leaks, the taps generated "a wealth of information," which was transcribed and turned over to the White House, "about the personal lives of the targets—their social contacts, their vacation plans . . . marital problems . . . drinking habits, and even their sex lives." In addition, purely political information was obtained from the phones of two targets who were advisers to Senators Edmund Muskie and Edward Kennedy. These taps on newsmen and executive officials were merely the successors to taps in the early and mid-1960s on other newsmen, including Hanson W. Baldwin of the *New York Times* in an always futile effort to ascertain the sources of leaks. . . .

These are but a few of many. Attorney General Edward Levi reported that from 1940 to 1975, the FBI alone had installed some 10,000 taps and bugs. This is probably but a small portion of the surveillance that actually took place, if one considers the activities of the CIA, the NSA, the IRS, the military, and some 20 other federal agencies which conduct electronic surveillance, about which Levi did not testify. The CIA, for example, has admitted tapping people it considered left-wingers both in this country and abroad, partly in something called Operation CHAOS, an effort to find links between anti-war groups in this country and foreign groups, which were never found; the National Security Agency has intercepted millions of overseas telegram and telephone messages; the military listened in on numerous radio messages in the late 1960s and early 1970s in connection with civil disorders and in full knowledge that such listening was illegal. And the FBI may not have reported all the taps and bugs it installed; in various court proceedings, such as the *Wounded Knee* and *Socialist Workers Party* cases, the courts have found that the FBI had lied about the existence of taps and bugs. In addition to all this, there are an unknown number installed by local police "Red" squads, often at the instigation of federal officers.

In the Name of National Security

All of this was done in the name of national security. In reality, it was aimed again and again at dissent and association. The FBI, for example, saw itself as "the guardian of public order" and established values, ordained "to maintain the existing social and political order." As the Church Committee put it, "the Bureau chose sides in the major social movements of the last 15 years and then attacked the other side with the unchecked power at its disposal." The very vagueness of the targets of FBI and other investigations makes this clear. The FBI and other national security agencies set up and indexed files and spied on people it considered "rabble rousers," "agitators," "subversives," "Black nationalists," "dissidents," "radical left," "new left," "extremists," "communist infiltrators," and the like. In many cases, these were citizens who simply disagreed with government policies.

And what was the primary purpose? To get names and to amass files on "enemies," people with whom the agencies were at "war." As one senior FBi official put it: "No holds were barred. We have used [similar] techniques against Soviet agents [The same methods were] brought home against any organization against which we were targeted. We did not differentiate. This is a rough, tough business. . . . Legality was not questioned, it was not an issue.". . .

Does Surveillance Serve a Purpose?

What good has all this tapping and bugging of law-abiding Americans done? Very little. Although the primary purpose of all intelligence surveillance is supposed to be preventive, both the National Wiretap Commission and the Church Committee make it clear that such successes are rare indeed. The Wiretap Commission offered a few examples of successful prevention where domestic criminality is concerned, and the Church Committee simply said that preventive intelligence had occasionally been useful for national security, but it specified nothing about whether the electronic surveillance had contributed to that utility.

Many who have worked with national security surveillance have disparaged its value. . . . Ramsey Clark declared in 1972 that if all national security intelligence taps were turned off, the net adverse impact on national security would be "absolutely zero." Morton Halperin, a former staff member of the National Security Council, has taken the same position. CIA records disclosed that its microphone surveillance of Micronesian officials was "wholly unproductive," according to a Senate Intelligence Committee report in April 1977. The Court of Appeals for the Third Circuit found that the taps in one case had been "ineffective and unsuccessful," and the JDL taps did not prevent an Amtorg office bombing. The Church Committee concluded that wiretapping and bugging had been particularly useless with respect to discovering the sources of leaks, despite repeated use of electronic surveillance for this purpose by several Administrations. And many intelligence experts have consistently downgraded the importance of any kind of covert intelligence gathering. William F. Sullivan, former assistant to J. Edgar Hoover for Intelligence, has even suggested prohibiting all electronic surveillance for a trial period of three years to see how we would manage; obviously, he doesn't think the Republic would totter during those three years. The Church Committee opposed electronic surveillance of Americans for purely intelligence purposes, and proposed that no non-consensual electronic surveillance of Americans be conducted except under Title III, with somewhat looser provisions for surveillance of foreigners, and an amendment of the espionage laws to include "industrial and other modern forms of espionage."

Cutting across all of this is a lesson history has taught again and again. From the Alien and Sedition Laws to Watergate, it is clear that executive power cannot be trusted, that it constantly identifies national security with personal political security, and that especially in times of stress, the courts cannot be relied upon to curb it. Nor can we rely on good people in office. It really doesn't make much difference who is in power. Once in office Jefferson, Lincoln, Wilson, Roosevelt, Truman, Eisenhower, Kennedy, and Johnson all committed grave violations of civil liberties when they felt threatened. No executive, caught in one of our perpetual domestic or international crises, can be expected to resist the temptation to use all the power at his disposal to fight criticism or obstruction of what he thinks he must do for what he may honestly consider the common good.

Legislation on Intelligence Surveillance

Any legislation to authorize intelligence surveillance must therefore be scrutinized very carefully, for the power it grants will almost certainly be stretched to the utmost. There is no reason to allow intelligence surveillance for domestic purposes, and neither the National Wiretap Commission nor the Justice Department has suggested it. Where foreign intelligence surveillance is concerned, no case has been made for going beyond the Church Committee recommendations mentioned above. . . .

Intelligence surveillance is something new in American law, and quite dangerous. Mechanically and legally, it is very difficult to control, especially where the investigations in which it is used are for such broad and vague purposes as national security or "foreign policy."

Nor dare we forget that more than wiretapping is involved. The electronic eavesdropping we authorize in the name of national security will not stop with that kind of "dirty business." The same justification has been applied to break-ins, burglaries, and physical violence by the intelligence agencies. It will be again.

READING

20 COVERT ACTION AND INTELLIGENCE

PRESENT LAWS PROTECT LIBERTY

William H. Webster

William H. Webster presented the following testimony in his capacity as Director of Central Intelligence. Prior to that he served as Director of the FBI, as judge for the United States Court of Appeals for the Eighth Circuit, and as a U.S. Attorney for the Eastern District of Missouri.

Points to Consider:

1. Why does the author believe that new intelligence legislation is unnecessary?
2. What steps did the President take to improve procedures?
3. Summarize the author's opinion of the Iran/Contra matter.

Excerpted from the testimony of William H. Webster before the House Subcommittee on Legislation of the Permanent Select Committee on Intelligence, February 24, 1988.

I am convinced that the current framework, and not new laws, represents the most appropriate and effective means to achieve our shared commitment to have Congress play an active, effective role in the oversight of United States intelligence activities.

I am pleased to be here today to share some of my thoughts on H.R. 3822, the Intelligence Oversight Act of 1987. The views expressed in this statement also reflect the position of the Administration with respect to the issues my statement addresses. . . . I would also draw your attention to the Administration's position, as conveyed to Congress in the President's legislative message last month, that a bill which fails to preserve the flexibility and authority the President needs to conduct intelligence activities effectively will not be acceptable to the President.

The bill being considered by the Committee today is similar in many respects to a bill reported out of the Senate Intelligence Committee last month. During its consideration of that bill, the Senate Intelligence Committee invited me to provide my views. I testified at that time on two issues: whether legislation was necessary, and what practical impact the Senate bill would have on the intelligence community. I intend to address both points in my testimony today on the House bill.

The Need for Legislation

As you are probably now aware, in my remarks before the Senate Intelligence Committee I questioned the need for this type of legislation. Although the Senate Intelligence Committee subsequently decided to recommend approval of the legislation, I still strongly doubt that this legislation is a necessary response to the concerns members of Congress have expressed about the oversight of special activities. As you know, the President recognized last spring that there was room for improvement in the way the two branches were meeting their responsibilities, and he took concrete, substantial steps to establish improved procedures to ensure that Congress is given the opportunity to play its appropriate oversight role. These new procedures in the form of a new National Security Decision Directive on Special Activities (NSDD 286), which this Committee has had for review in full and much of which was recently declassified, clarify the rules by which special activities are reviewed, approved, and reported to Congress. In fact, many of the proposals contained in H.R. 3822 are already contained in NSDD 286. That is not

> ## VIGOROUS ENFORCEMENT
>
> *The FBI remains committed to the vigorous enforcement of the nation's civil rights laws. We shall examine each incident as it is brought to light and be alert for facts indicating a civil rights offense or other wrongdoing. We shall respond in a professional manner in those instances in which we have investigative jurisdiction.*
>
> Excerpted from the testimony of Oliver B. Revell, Executive Assistant Director of the FBI, before the House Judiciary Committee, February 19, 1987

surprising, because the procedures the President has installed were developed following close and prolonged consultation with members and staffs of the intelligence committees.

While a Presidential Directive is not the same as legislation, I am not persuaded that new legislation at this time is the best way to address the concerns that members have with the congressional role regarding special activities. In my view, a legislative remedy should be employed only if it is clear that there is a basic deficiency in the oversight process. That is doubly the case when the legislative remedy proposed raises constitutional issues which threaten to divide the two branches in an area where effective work places a premium on cooperation.

The Intelligence Community

The Iran/Contra matter, while extremely serious, has not in my view demonstrated that the system of congressional oversight of the intelligence community established under current statutes is seriously flawed. Many of the problems exposed in connection with that unfortunate period were the result of officials failing to follow existing procedures and rules. As the Committee is aware, I have taken steps within the CIA to discipline those employees who failed to follow CIA procedures and meet the standards of conduct expected of CIA employees or who testified to Congress in a manner that was not candid or forthcoming. Those actions, taken in light of the requirements defined by current statute, in my view have adequately addressed the problems we found. Similarly, to the extent that there were any procedural shortcomings demonstrated by the Iran/Contra matter, they have already been addressed by the new Presidential Directive within the present statutory framework.

I would like to emphasize that any legislation that is enacted must not adversely affect the intelligence community's ability to do its job. In this connection, the bill you introduced, and the bill reported out of the Senate Intelligence Committee, have sought to address constructively some of the important concerns I and other Administration officials raised before the Senate Intelligence Committee when it considered its original bill. That bill, for examples, recognizes the need to report on special activities and intelligence collection in a manner consistent with due regard for the protection of sensitive intelligence sources and methods. I am also pleased that neither the House nor the Senate bills require that the finding specify the identity of foreign countries assisting the agency in the conduct of special activities. The proviso on protection of sources and methods, and the ability to protect the identity of foreign countries assisting us will go a long way in assuring friendly services and potential agents that source-identifying information will not be widely disseminated and possibly compromised. . . .

Conclusion

In closing, I would like to reemphasize my personal commitment to making the oversight process work. It has always been clear, and recent experience has again demonstrated that the implementation of the foreign policy of our government, including special activities, can only be successful when the Executive and Legislative branches of government work together in an atmosphere of mutual respect and trust. This spirit of cooperation can only occur if the intelligence committees receive the appropriate information needed to review and make informed judgments on special activities, while at the same time ensuring that this information is protected from unauthorized disclosure. The law should reflect not only the need for cooperation, but also the President's responsibility for the conduct and management of our intelligence and the importance to the nation of ensuring that the President has the necessary flexibility and authority to employ our intelligence capability effectively.

As I have noted, the President has taken corrective steps to improve the oversight system through a Presidential Directive. At the CIA, I have approved a number of measures which will help to prevent a repetition of the shortcomings in the agency's performance in the Iran/Contra matter. In short, significant changes have been made. I would respectfully submit that they should be given a chance to work. I am convinced that the current framework, and not new laws, represents the most appropriate and effective means to achieve our shared commitment to have Congress play an active, effective role in the oversight of United States intelligence activities.

READING

21 COVERT ACTION AND INTELLIGENCE

FORSAKING DEMOCRACY: THE COLD WAR AND COVERT ACTION

Eric Black

Eric Black wrote this article in his capacity as a staff writer for the Star Tribune, *a daily newspaper of the Minneapolis and St. Paul, Minnesota area.*

Points to Consider:

1. Who is George Kennan? What was his warning?
2. Describe what happened when Guatemala tried to help the peasants through land reform.
3. How did the CIA assist in overthrowing the Guatemalan government?
4. What is the Cold War mentality?

Eric Black, "Forsaking Democracy," *Star Tribune*, September 12, 1988. Reprinted with permission from the *Star Tribune*, Minneapolis-St. Paul.

The Cold War has presented the United States with many situations where it had to choose whether to foster democracy or fight communism. In almost every instance, the United States has forsaken democracy.

The United States likes to think of itself as a force for democracy in the world, as well as the leader in the Cold War fight against communism.

When we could fight communism by siding with democratic regimes, we have done so, as with the Marshall Plan's aid to Western Europe after World War II.

The Cold War, however, has presented the United States with many situations where it had to choose whether to foster democracy or fight communism. In almost every instance, the United States has forsaken democracy.

Forsaking Democracy

Pakistan President Muhammad Zia ul-Haq, killed last month in a plane crash, overthrew a democratic regime by force in 1977. The United States befriended and aided him anyway because he was a staunch anti-Communist in a strategic location. South Africa deprives most of its citizens of basic liberties. The United States has remained friendly, defending its policy on a Cold War rationale. Former Philippines dictator Ferdinand Marcos and the military regime in South Korea retained U.S. support and friendship long after they had revealed themselves as dictatorships.

Siding with undemocratic elements when there is no democratic element in the picture is one thing. But the ugliest cases have been those in which the United States helped overthrow democratic regimes. George Kennan, the father of the U.S. containment policy, once warned that if, in the name of fighting communism, the United States overthrew an elected government, it would "have a demoralizing influence on our whole foreign policy and corrupt that basic decency of purpose which, despite all our blunders and our shortsightedness, still makes us a great figure among the nations of the world."

In 1954, in Guatemala, the United States betrayed its self-image as the friend of democracy. By overthrowing the elected government of Guatemala and replacing it with a brutal military dictatorship, the United States played the role of international bully and slayer of democracy. The case was

> **SECRET GOVERNMENT**
>
> *Some of President Reagan's top advisers operated a parallel government that, among other things, has been linked to the theft of briefing materials from Jimmy Carter's 1980 presidential campaign. . . .*
>
> *The group operated outside the traditional Cabinet departments and agencies almost from the day Reagan took office, with the National Security Council coordinating its activities, congressional investigators and administration officials told The Miami Herald. . . .*
>
> *The newspaper quoted one unidentified source as saying that the influence of fired National Security Council aide Oliver North was so great that he was able to have the orbits of surveillance satellites altered to follow Soviet ships around the world and called for the launching of high-flying spy aircraft on secret missions over Cuba and Nicaragua.*
>
> *North also was said to have drafted a secret contingency plan that called for suspension of the Constitution, turning control of the United States over to the Federal Emergency Management Agency, appointment of military commanders to run state and local government and declaration of martial law during a national crisis, the Herald said.*
>
> "Report Claims U.S. Had 'Secret Government'," Minneapolis Star Tribune, July 5, 1987

doubly tragic because the supposedly Communist regime that the United States overthrew wasn't a Communist regime at all.

Trouble in Guatemala

Guatemala, the northernmost and most populous nation in Central America, suffered through the 1930s under a particularly cruel and vain little dictator named Jorge Ubico y Castaneda. Despite the brutality of his regime, Ubico maintained good relations with and received military aid from the United States.

In 1944 Guatemala enjoyed one of those outbursts of democracy that have occasionally decorated Latin American history. A nearly bloodless revolution (about 100 casualties), led by university students and the middle class, forced Ubico from power.

Philosopher and educator Juan Jose Arevalo Bermej was

elected president. Arevalo rejected Marxism, but called himself a "spiritual socialist." His top priority was establishing democracy.

Rather than welcoming the democratization of Guatemala, the U.S. government viewed it with suspicion. Arevalo was not a Communist, but he was less amenable to suggestions from Washington than Ubico had been. President Harry Truman cut off U.S. military aid.

Arevalo's successor, Jacobo Arbenz Guzman, received more than 60 percent of the vote in the 1950 elections.

The disparity between rich and poor in Guatemala was shocking even by Latin American standards. Although the majority of the population were Mayan Indians, the economy and political structure were dominated by a small class of super-rich Europeans. Two percent of the population owned 70 percent of the land. While the landless peasants starved, half of the arable land was left fallow by the choice of the richest landowners.

Land Reform Law

In 1952 Arbenz put through a land reform law designed to help the peasants escape from grinding poverty while still respecting the fundamental capitalist structure. Under the program, land would be taken from the biggest farms, but only land that was uncultivated. The owners would be compensated on the basis of the value of the land on the tax rolls. The 1.6 million acres expropriated under this program was distributed to about 87,000 Guatemalans, most of them Mayans. Some of the new Mayan holdings were converted into communal farms.

The U.S.-based United Fruit Co., the world's biggest producer of bananas, was the largest landowner in Guatemala. Of its 550,000 acres, only 15 percent were under cultivation. By 1954, more than 400,000 of United Fruit's acres had been expropriated. True to the letter of its law, the Guatemalan government offered to pay United Fruit $1.18 million—the exact amount United Fruit had declared its land to be worth on Guatemalan tax records. Through their cozy relationship with previous regimes, major Guatemalan landowners had been permitted to grossly undervalue their lands so taxes would be lower.

United Fruit launched a successful lobbying and public relations campaign to convince the U.S. government and public that communism had taken over in Guatemala.

"First they claim the government never listens to them— then they complain when we use a little electronic surveillance."

Illustration by Carol* Simpson.

By the time Dwight Eisenhower took office in 1953, Communist domination of the Guatemalan government was treated as an established fact. A memo to the U.S. Cabinet said, "Timely action is extremely desirable to prevent communism from spreading seriously beyond Guatemala."

Blind to Kennan's warning, the U.S. government undertook a covert operation to overthrow the only democratic regime in Central America.

Counterrevolution Takes Place

A veteran anti-Communist diplomat, John Peurifoy, was assigned to Guatemala as the U.S. ambassador and to serve as point man for the plot. The CIA chose a Guatemalan expatriate, Carlos Enrique Castillo-Armas, to lead the insurgency. The dictators of Honduras and Nicaragua cooperated and offered training bases. The CIA trained and equipped a small force in

Honduras.

Arbenz learned of the training activities. The United States had successfully pressured its European allies not to sell arms to Guatemala. Desperate for arms to defend itself, the Arbenz government arranged a secret shipment of arms from Czechoslovakia in May 1954. U.S. intelligence spotted the shipment and publicized it as proof that Guatemala was in the Communist camp.

The overthrow in June 1954 was farcical. Castillo-Armas had only 300 troops and two obsolete U.S. bombers (flown by U.S. pilots). He crossed the border into Guatemala June 17 and established a camp. The idea was that he would announce he had arrived to liberate his homeland, and volunteers would throng to his banner. No one thronged.

A propaganda team trained and funded by the CIA beamed radio broadcasts into Guatemala City announcing that a large and invincible force was marching toward the capital. In reality, Castillo-Armas sat in his camp and waited. But the Yankee pilots in the U.S.-supplied planes made enough loud explosions in and near the capital to convince the population that the radio broadcasts were true.

Seeing signs that the Guatemalan army's loyalty to him was wavering, Arbenz panicked. He ordered the military to distribute arms to the population so a militia could be formed. The military chief refused, and told Arbenz to resign or seek truce talks with Castillo-Armas.

Castillo-Armas Rises to Power

Arbenz was finished either way. He turned over power to his military chief. Under pressure from U.S. Ambassador Peurifoy, the army agreed to let Castillo-Armas march into the capital. Also at Peurifoy's insistence, Castillo-Armas was made acting president. In what you might call a highly supervised election, the man whom the CIA had chosen to run Guatemala was elected three months later with 99 percent of the vote.

Castillo-Armas returned 99 percent of United Fruit's confiscated land to the company. His government returned most of the rest of the redistributed land to its pre-Arbenz owners. To cleanse Guatemala of all signs of support for the former revolution, Castillo-Armas imprisoned thousands of former supporters of the Arbenz regime.

Castillo-Armas visited the United States the following year. He received a 21-gun salute in Washington, D.C., a ticker-tape parade in New York and honorary degrees from Fordham and Columbia universities, and paid a visit to the hospital bed where Eisenhower was recovering from a heart attack.

Throughout his tour, he was treated as the hero who had defeated communism and restored freedom in Guatemala. Although the CIA role did not come to light for many years, the Eisenhower administration treated the defeat of communism in Guatemala as one of its greatest foreign policy accomplishments. Neither then nor later did it produce proof that what it had overthrown had been a Communist or Soviet-oriented regime.

That's because Arbenz was not a Communist. He was a nationalist who had gained power democratically on the tide of a middle-class revolution.

Yes, there were a few thousand Communists in Guatemala, most of whom supported Arbenz. Yes, one of Guatemala's minor political parties was controlled by Communists, but it never filled more than four seats in the 56-member National Assembly.

No evidence has emerged to show that Communists held key positions in the government or the army, nor that they were influential in shaping Arbenz's program, nor that the Soviet Union dominated the Guatemalan government or even controlled the Guatemalan Communists.

In retrospect, it appears that Arbenz's program was designed to address the very conditions of poverty, hopelessness, authoritarianism and foreign domination that have been breeding grounds for communism in the Third World.

The Cold War Mentality

How could the United States have been so wrong about Arbenz?

Those who believe that the U.S. Cold War policy is a tool of big corporations make great use of the Guatemalan intervention. John Foster Dulles, the secretary of state who helped conceive the operation, and his brother, Allen Dulles, the CIA director who helped execute it, were United Fruit stockholders. Their former law firm represented United Fruit. Certainly United Fruit wanted Arbenz overthrown.

But to portray the intervention as a straightforward bailout of United Fruit is an oversimplification. The motives for the operation lay deeper. As the Cold War mentality took hold, any Latin American government that sought independence from the

United States was suspected of Communist leanings. Secretary Dulles argued that neutrality in the Cold War was immoral.

Arbenz tolerated Communists but wasn't controlled by them. His land reform program seems moderate compared with the Cuban expropriations of the 1960s. The communal farms were a reflection of centuries-old Mayan tradition, not modeled on Soviet agriculture. Arbenz sought arms from Czechoslovakia only after the United States had cut off alternative sources. But in the Cold War hysteria of the 1950s, such fine distinctions were not made.

The CIA overthrow of Arbenz was not the first or last time the United States helped snuff out a democracy. The year before Guatemala, the CIA undermined the parliamentary-style government of Mohammad Mossadegh in Iran and put the autocratic shah in power. The degree of direct U.S. complicity in the 1971 assassination of President Salvador Allende of Chile remains disputed. It appears that the CIA did not commission the coup, as it had in Iran and Guatemala, but the U.S. government was the enemy of that elected regime.

Neither Iran nor Chile has had a political democracy since. Guatemala has suffered through a succession of military dictatorships, all befriended by the United States. The concentration of wealth remains almost as extreme as ever. The horrible Latin American traditions of "death squads" and *desaparecidos* ("the disappeared ones") originated in Guatemala in the 1960s. Since 1966, 38,000 people have "disappeared" and at least 100,000 Guatemalans have been executed.

Since the 1986 inauguration of a new civilian president, Vinicio Cerezo, the United States has called Guatemala one of the "emerging democracies" of the region. Death squad activity declined briefly after Cerezo's election, but seems to be rising again. Cerezo can't control it because he can't control the army.

Cerezo survived a recent coup attempt, but his grasp on the presidency is tenuous. He knows that if he displeases the military leadership by trying to reform Guatemala too fast, he won't last.

READING

22 COVERT ACTION AND INTELLIGENCE

PROTECTING DEMOCRACY: INTELLIGENCE AND COVERT ACTIONS IN HISTORY

The Minority Report of the Iran-Contra Affair

This reading was excerpted from the Minority Report of the Report of the Congressional Committees Investigating the Iran-Contra Affair. The report includes findings, conclusions, and recommendations, together with supplemental, minority, and additional views.

Points to Consider:

1. What information did the Committee of Secret Correspondence refuse to tell Congress?

2. Describe President Washington's "secret service" fund.

3. Why did the Madison Administration use "secret agents"?

4. How was President Pierce's plan to acquire Cuba from Spain foiled?

Excerpted from The Minority Report in *Report of the Congressional Committees Investigating the Iran-Contra Affair,* 100th Congress, 1st Session. U.S. Government Printing Office, Washington, D.C., 1987, pp. 467-469.

During the country's first century, Presidents used literally hundreds of secret agents at their own discretion.

Intelligence and Covert Actions Throughout History

We end this review of historical precedent with a brief overview of intelligence and covert actions authorized by past Presidents. That history begins in the earliest days of the nation. As Representative Hyde mentioned during Admiral Poindexter's testimony on July 17, [1] the Continental Congress—which did not have a separate executive branch—set up a Committee of Secret Correspondence made up of Benjamin Franklin, Robert Morris, Benjamin Harrison, John Dickinson, and John Jay. On October 1, 1776, Franklin and Morris were told that France would be willing to extend credit to the revolutionaries to help them buy arms. They wrote:

> Considering the nature and importance of [the above intelligence,] we agree in opinion that it is our indispensable duty to keep it a secret from Congress. . . . As the court of France has taken measures to negotiate this loan in the most cautious and secret manner, should we divulge it immediately we may not only lose the present benefit but also render the court cautious of any further connection with such unguarded people and prevent their granting other loans of assistance that we stand in need of. [2]

In a subsequent chapter on leaks, we shall discuss the methods this committee used to protect secrets, some of which should be revived today.

The Important Role of Intelligence

The *Federalist* also recognized the important role intelligence might play under the new Constitution. *Federalist* No. 64, about treaties, was written by Jay, an experienced diplomat as well as a former member of the Committee on Secret Correspondence. He said:

> It seldom happens in the negotiation of treaties, of whatever nature, but that perfect secrecy and immediate dispatch are sometimes requisite. There are cases when the most useful intelligence may be obtained, if the person possessing it can be relieved from apprehensions of discovery. Those apprehensions will operate on those persons whether they are actuated by mercenary or friendly motives; and there are doubtless many of both descriptions who would rely on the

> **COVERT ACTIONS**
>
> *Since the mid-1970s, Congress has had a direct role in overseeing covert actions engaged in by the CIA and other entities of the U.S. intelligence community. Covert actions or "special activities" have traditionally included secret political, economic, propaganda, and paramilitary activities designed to influence foreign governments, organizations, or events in support of U.S. foreign policy objectives. They are planned and executed so that the role of the U.S. government is not apparent or acknowledged publicly. Such operations have been controversial in the post-Vietnam War period but Congress and the executive branch have seen them as a potentially useful adjunct to U.S. foreign policy.*
>
> Richard F. Grimmett, Covert Actions: Congressional Oversight, *January 19, 1989, Congressional Research Service Issue Brief, The Liberty of Congress, Washington, D.C.*

secrecy of the President, but who would not confide in that of the Senate, and still less in that of a large popular assembly. The convention have done well therefore in so disposing of the power of making treaties, that although the President must in forming them act by the advice and consent of the senate, yet he will be able to manage the business of intelligence in such a manner as prudence may suggest.[3]

The Use of "Special Agents"

Beginning with George Washington, almost every President has used "special agents" — people, often private individuals, appointed for missions by the President without Senate confirmation — to help gain the intelligence about which Jay wrote, and to engage in a broad range of other activities with or against foreign countries. The first such agent was Gouverneur Morris, who was sent to Great Britain in 1789 to explore the chances for opening normal diplomatic communications.[4] At the same time, Britain sent a "private agent" to the United States who communicated outside normal channels through Secretary of Treasury Alexander Hamilton instead of through the Francophile Secretary of State, Thomas Jefferson.[5] Washington's agents were paid from a "secret service" fund he was allowed to use at his discretion, without detailed accounting.[6]

Covert Activity in the Madison Administration

The early examples that are most interesting for these investigations are ones in which the President used his discretionary power to authorize covert actions ("Covert action" is an inexact term generally recognized to include covert political action, covert propaganda, intelligence deception, and covert paramilitary assistance.) In the period of 1810-12, for example, Madison used agents to stimulate revolts in East and West Florida that eventually led to an overt, Congressionally unauthorized military force to gain U.S. control over territories held by a country with which the United States was at peace. Even more telling, however, is the following example from the Madison Administration.

> Madison [in 1810] sent Joel R. Poinsett, secretly and without Senate approval, to South America as an agent for seamen and commerce. Poinsett did some commercial work, but he broadly construed instructions from Secretaries of State Smith and Monroe, and worked intimately with revolutionary leaders in Argentina and Chile, suggesting commercial and military plans, helping them obtain arms, and actually leading a division of the Chilean army against Peruvian loyalists. Nothing in Poinsett's instructions specifically authorized these activities. But he had kept the administration advised of most of his plans and received virtually no directions for long periods of time, and no orders to refrain in any way from aiding the revolutionaries . . . Poinsett was given broad leeway to advance the republican cause, without any commitment from the administration. He was told to write in code, and all his important communications were withheld from Congress.[7]

In other words, Poinsett made Oliver North look like a piker.

More Examples of Early Covert Activity

In 1843, President Tyler secretly sent Duff Green to Great Britain to engage in secret propaganda activities relating to the U.S. desire to annex Texas. At one point, Green had a letter published in a newspaper without using his own name. This raised a furor among members of Congress, several of whom demanded to know his identity. Because Green was paid out of the President's contingency fund, Congress made the fund an issue during the subsequent administration of President Polk. Polk refused to disclose his expenditures in a statement that

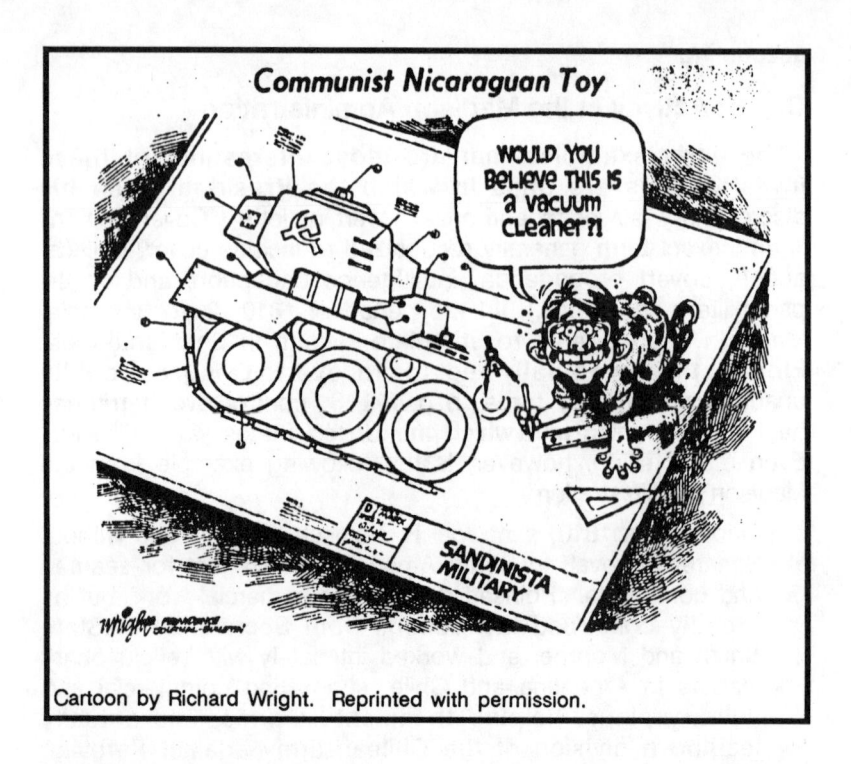

Cartoon by Richard Wright. Reprinted with permission.

openly acknowledged they were being used for more than intelligence gathering:

> In no nation is the application of such funds to be made public. In time of war or impending danger the situation of the country will make it necessary to employ individuals for the purpose of obtaining information *or rendering other important services* who could never be prevailed upon to act if they entertained the least apprehension that their names or their agency would in any contingency be revealed. [8]

One early example of a covert action brought to an end through a leak is described in Edward Sayle's article on the history of U.S. intelligence:

> President Pierce, as Polk, made extensive use of agents and covert action. One of the most innovative plans was to acquire Cuba from Spain. Spain had refused to part with the troublesome island, and a scheme was devised to force them to sell. It called for cooperative European money-lenders to call in their loans to the Spanish Crown, pressuring Madrid to sell Cuba to the United States as a means to raise the needed cash. The plan went well until leaked to the *New York Herald*. [9]

Examples like these are legion. During the country's first century, Presidents used literally hundreds of secret agents at their own discretion. Congress did give the President a contingency fund for these agents, but never specifically approved, or was asked to approve any particular agent or activity. In fact, Congress never approved or was asked to approve covert activity in general. The Presidents were simply using their inherent executive powers under Article II of the Constitution. For the Congresses that had accepted the overt presidential uses of military force summarized in the previous section, the use of Executive power for these kinds of covert activities raised no constitutional questions.

Conclusion

Presidents asserted their constitutional independence from Congress early. They engaged in secret diplomacy and intelligence activities, and refused to share the results with Congress if they saw fit. They unilaterally established U.S. military and diplomatic policy with respect to foreign belligerent states, in quarrels involving the United States, and in quarrels involving only third parties. They enforced this policy abroad, using force if necessary. They engaged U.S. troops abroad to serve American interests without congressional approval, and in a number of cases apparently against explicit directions from Congress. They also had agents engage in what would commonly be referred to as covert actions, again without Congressional approval. In short, Presidents exercised a broad range of foreign policy powers for which they neither sought nor received Congressional sanction through statute.

This history speaks volumes about the Constitution's allocation of powers between the branches. It leaves little, if any, doubt that the President was expected to have the primary role of conducting the foreign policy of the United States. Congressional actions to limit the President in this area therefore should be reviewed with a considerable degree of skepticism. If they interfere with core presidential foreign policy functions, they should be struck down. Moreover, the lesson of our constitutional history is that doubtful cases should be decided in favor of the President. [10]

---

[1] Hearings, July 17, pp. 205-07.

[2] Revolutionary Diplomatic Correspondence of the United

States, October 1, 1776.

[3] Federalist No. 64 at 434-35, emphasis in the original.

[4] U.S. Senate, 94th Cong., 2d Sess., Select Committee to Study Governmental Operations with Respect to Intelligence Activities, Final Report: Foreign and Military Intelligence, S.Rept. 94-755 (1976), Book I, p. 34.

[5] Leonard D. White, The Federalists: A Study in Administrative History, 1789-1801 (1948), pp. 212-13.

[6] 1 Stat. 128-29. See also, L. White, The Federalists at 343; Sayle, "Historical Underpinnings," at 9.

[7] Sofaer, War, Foreign Affairs and the Constitution at 264-65.

[8] As quoted by Sayle, "Historical Underpinnings," at 15.

[9] Sayle, "Historical Underpinnings," at 16.

[10] See letter from John Norton Moore to Brendan Sullivan, July 9, 1987, p. 2, reprinted at the end of the minority report.

Reading and Reasoning

WHAT IS POLITICAL BIAS?

This activity may be used as an individualized study guide for students in libraries and resource centers or as a discussion catalyst in small group and classroom discussions.

Many readers are unaware that written material usually expresses an opinion or bias. The skill to read with insight and understanding requires the ability to detect different kinds of bias. Political bias, race bias, sex bias, ethnocentric bias, and religious bias are five basic kinds of opinions expressed in editorials and literature that attempts to persuade. This activity will focus on political bias, defined in the glossary below.

Five Kinds of Editorial Opinion or Bias

SEX BIAS—The expression of dislike for and/or feeling of superiority over the opposite sex or a particular sexual minority.

RACE BIAS—The expression of dislike for and/or feeling of superiority over a racial group.

ETHNOCENTRIC BIAS—The expression of a belief that one's own group, race, religion, culture, or nation is superior. Ethnocentric persons judge others by their own standards and values.

POLITICAL BIAS—The expression of political opinions and attitudes about domestic or foreign affairs.

RELIGIOUS BIAS—The expression of a religious belief or attitude.

Guidelines

Read through the following statements and decide which ones represent political opinions or bias. Evaluate each statement by using the method indicated.

- Place the letter [P] in front of any sentence that reflects political opinion or bias
- Place the letter [N] in front of any sentence that does not reflect political opinion or bias
- Place the letter [S] in front of any sentence that you are not sure about.

1. Where national security is concerned, privacy and confidentiality have rarely carried much weight.

2. The FBI sees itself as the "guardian of public order."

3. Intelligence surveillance is even more indiscriminate and inclusive than law-enforcement surveillance.

4. If all national security intelligence taps were turned off, the net adverse impact on national security would be "absolutely zero."

5. Throughout history, several presidents have committed grave violations of civil liberties when they felt threatened.

6. Intelligence surveillance is something new in American law, and quite dangerous.

7. For years now, the CIA and the National Security Council have been skirting the law, trying to achieve by covert action what they cannot justify or explain to Congress.

8. The United States likes to think of itself as a force for democracy in the world, as well as the leader in the Cold War fight against communism.

9. Congress has had a direct role in overseeing covert actions.

10. Mechanically and legally, it is difficult to control intelligence surveillance, especially where the investigations are used for such broad and vague purposes as national security or "foreign policy."

Other Activities

1. Locate three examples of political opinion or bias in the readings from Chapter Five.

2. Make up one statement that would be an example of each of the following: *sex bias, race bias, ethnocentric bias, and religious bias.*

3. See if you can locate any factual statements in the ten items listed above.

APPENDIX

Definitions of Key Terms

The following terms are widely used in this book and subject to a range of interpretations: intelligence, the intelligence community, and covert or special action. Sample definitions appear below.

Intelligence

A concise definition of intelligence was provided by a task force of the second Hoover Commission, whose members were appointed jointly by President Eisenhower and leading members of Congress in 1955: "Intelligence deals with all things which should be known in advance of initiating a course of action."[1]

The same task force also made use of a more detailed definition contained in the Dictionary of United States Military Terms for Joint Usage: *"Intelligence—The product resulting from collection, evaluation, analysis, integration and interpretation of all available information which concerns one or more aspects of foreign nations or of areas of operations, and which is immediately or potentially significant to planning."*[2]

The Church Committee in 1976 employed a similar but more abbreviated definition: *"Intelligence*: The product resulting from the collection, collation, evaluation, analysis, integration, and interpretation of all collected information."[3]

Intelligence Community

The intelligence community is defined in President Reagan's Executive Order 12333 as consisting of the following agencies or organizations: the Central Intelligence Agency (CIA); the National Security Agency (NSA); the Defense Intelligence Agency (DIA); the offices within the Department of Defense for the collection of specialized foreign intelligence through reconnaissance programs; the Bureau of Intelligence and Research of the Department of State; the intelligence elements of the Army, Navy, Air Force, and Marine Corps, the Federal Bureau of Investigation (FBI), the Department of the Treasury, and the Department of Energy; and the staff elements of the Director of Central Intelligence.[4] A largely similar definition was provided by President Carter's earlier Executive Order 12036.

There are no clear statutory definitions of the intelligence community.

Covert or Special Action

This term is subject to a wide range of interpretations. Strictly speaking, covert (or special) actions fall outside the scope of most definitions of intelligence, including those cited above. Covert actions are often associated with the intelligence community, particularly the CIA; however, they comprise only a small part of the activities of intelligence agencies, which are primarily concerned with the routine collection and analysis of information.

A broad definition of covert action is suggested in the wording of the Hughes-Ryan Amendment (1974) to the Foreign Assistance Act of 1961. The Hughes-Ryan Amendment does not specifically mention covert, or special, action; however, the following excerpt as highlighted in bold type is sometimes cited as an implicit definition: "No funds appropriated under the authority of this chapter or any other Act may be expended by or on behalf of the Central Intelligence Agency **for operations in foreign countries, other than activities intended solely for obtaining necessary intelligence,** unless and until the President finds that each such operation is important to the national security of the United States."

A somewhat more narrow definition is provided in Executive Order 12333, which refers to "special" rather than "covert" activities: "*Special activities* means activities conducted in support of national foreign policy objectives abroad which are planned and executed so that the role of the United States government is not apparent or acknowledged publicly, and functions in support of such activities, but which are not intended to influence United States political processes, public opinion, policies, or media and do not include diplomatic activities or the collection and production of intelligence or related support functions."[5]

The proposed Intelligence Oversight Act of 1988 (H.R. 3822) employs the term "covert action" and provides a more detailed definition in Section 503(e):

As used in this title, the term "covert action" means an activity or activities conducted by an element of the United States government to influence political, economic, or military conditions abroad so that the role of the United States government is not intended to be apparent or acknowledged publicly, but does not include—

(1) activities the primary purpose of which is to acquire intelligence, traditional counterintelligence activities, traditional activities to improve or maintain the operational security of United States government programs, or administrative activities;

(2) traditional diplomatic or military activities or routine support to such activities;

(3) traditional law enforcement activities conducted by United States government law enforcement agencies or routine support to such activities; or

(4) activities to provide routine support to the overt activities (other than activities described in paragraph (1), (2), or (3)) of other United States government agencies abroad.

A request by any department, agency, or entity of the United States to a foreign government or a private citizen to conduct a covert action on behalf of the United States shall be deemed to be a covert action.[6]

If this bill is enacted into law, it will provide the first clear statutory definition of covert action.

---

[1] Task Force on Intelligence Activities, Report on Intelligence Activities in the Federal Government. Part II of report by the Commission on Organization of the Executive Branch of the Government, Intelligence Activities: A Report to Congress. June 1955. p. 26

[2] Ibid.

[3] U.S. Congress. Senate. Final Report of the Select Committee to Study Governmental Operations with Respect to Intelligence Activities. Book I: Foreign and Military Intelligence. (Senate Report No. 94-755.) April 26, 1976. 94th Cong., 2d sess. Washington, U.S. Government Printing Office, 1976. p. 624.

[4] Executive Order 12333, December 4, 1981. Paragraph 3.4(f).

[5] Executive Order 12333, December 4, 1981. Paragraph 3.4(5)(h).

[6] U.S. Congress. House. Permanent Select Committee on Intelligence. Intelligence Oversight Act of 1988 (Report No. 100-705, Part I). June 15, 1988. 100th Cong., 2nd sess. Washington, U.S. Government Printing Office, 1988. p. 3. Also see Ibid., pp. 68-70 for views of the National Security Advisor on these definitions.

BIBLIOGRAPHY

Congress and Intelligence Policy

This bibliography presents literature on the role of Congress in oversight of intelligence operations. It examines recent issues arising from the Iran/Contra investigation as well as other topics.

Aberbach, Joel D. *The Congressional Committee Intelligence System: Information, Oversight, and Change.* Congress & the Presidency, v. 14, spring 1987: 51-76. LRS87-4253

Bamford, James. "Reagan CIA: Arrogance Instead of Oversight." *Los Angeles Times*, Jan. 4, 1987: 1, 6. LRS87-10264

"The Reagan Administration, on the one hand, pushed to the limit its involvement in covert wars, while on the other hand demonstrated only contempt for the whole principle of oversight. Although this attitude has been most obvious in the Administration's dealing with the congressional intelligence committees, it has also been a major factor in the virtual denigration of the important oversight and review panels in the executive branch itself."

Commager, Henry Steele. "'Intelligence': the Constitution Betrayed." *New York Review of Books*, Sept. 30, 1976: 32-34, 35-37. LRS76-14076

Condemns the President and intelligence community in the past decade for regarding themselves above the law and Constitution. Condemns the Congress for not exercising its constitutional obligation to oversee the intelligence community in the past two decades.

Durenberger, Dave. "Going Too Far: The President Needed the Intelligence Oversight Act." *Washington Post*, Nov. 24, 1986: A15. LRS86-14255

Outgoing Chairman of the Senate Intelligence Committee sets forth that "the Intelligence Oversight Act of 1980 did not spring whole from the head of Congress. It grew over time in response to actions by an executive branch that went too far. But intelligence oversight by Congress does not stand only on the potential it holds for curbing abuses by the executive. Equally important are the consultative values of oversight—to test and improve the quality of decisions and actions and to broaden the base of support under these decisions and actions."

Elliff, John T. "Congress and the Intelligence Community." In *Congress Reconsidered*. Edited by Lawrence C. Dodd and Bruce I. Oppenheimer. New York, Praeger, 1977. p. 193-206. LRS79-22170

"Recent experience demonstrates that Congress has the resources that, if used skillfully in the pursuit of an effective strategy, can win for it a share in control of the intelligence community. . . . Whatever may be the ultimate resolution of such issues as the procedures for oversight or the enactment of new legislative charters for the intelligence agencies, there has been a profound constitutional change in the relationship between Congress and the executive. Intelligence is no longer viewed as the exclusive domain of the executive branch."

Evans, Rowland. Novak, Robert. "Congress Is Crippling the CIA." *Reader's Digest,* v. 129, Nov. 1986: 99-103. LRS86-14252

"Charged with 'overseeing' U.S. intelligence, too many lawmakers, with too many political axes to grind, are leaking too many vital secrets. It's time to plug the holes."

Fisher, Louis. *The Legitimacy of the Congressional National Security Role.* S.1., 1987. 17, 2 p. LRS87-10269

In this paper, presented on Nov. 20, 1987 to the National Defense University, the author examines Reagan Administration action in Nicaragua, Lebanon, Grenada and Libya and then addresses such questions as "what may the President do pursuant to his express powers? What is added by so-called inherent or implied powers? What is the role of Congress? What statutory constraints operate on the President? Do we want the vague realm of 'national security' exercised solely by the President or through the collective efforts of the executive and legislative branches?"

Godson, Roy. "Congress and Foreign Intelligence." In *The CIA and the American Ethic, an Unfinished Debate,* edited by Ernest

W. Lefever and Roy Godson. Washington, Ethics and Public Policy Center, Georgetown University, 1979. p. 19-66. (Ethics and public policy studies) JK468.I6L43

"This chapter is divided into two parts. The first deals with legislation, congressional reorganization and oversight, and congressional efforts to improve the agencies' performance, to reform secrecy and disclosure procedures, and to enhance protection of the civil rights of U.S. citizens. The second part focuses on how Congress through public information and education has affected U.S. foreign intelligence capabilities."

Goodman, Allan E. "Reforming U.S. Intelligence." *Foreign Policy*, no. 67, summer 1987: 121-136. LRS87-3808

"The Iran-Contra affair is yet another demonstration that the integrity and effectiveness of the U.S. intelligence system have been substantially eroded by abuses stretching over many years and highlights the need for fundamental change in its management, operations, and control."

Grimmett, Richard F. *Covert Actions: Congressional Oversight: Issue Brief.* Regularly updated. Washington, Congressional Research Service, 1987. 14 p. IB87208

The "Iran-Contra affair" has focused legislature attention on the issue of congressional oversight of covert actions by the U.S. intelligence community.

Hamilton, Lee H. "Covert Actions Remain Necessary: We Need Only Careful Adherence to Existing Rules." *Los Angeles Times*, Nov. 22, 1987: 5. LRS87-10268

Chairman of the House Select Iran-Contra Committee examines the issue of covert operations. "The experience of the past decade has shown that this system governing covert operations can both protect secrets and provide accountability—if procedures are respected. In the Iran-Contra affair, they were not."

Intelligence Requirements for the 1980's. Edited by Roy Godson. Washington, National Strategy Information Center, c1979-1986. 7 v. UB251.U5I56

Volume 7 deals with Intelligence and public policy.

Johnson, Loch K. *A Season of Inquiry: the Senate Intelligence Investigation.* Lexington, Ky., University Press of Kentucky, 1985. 317 p. JK468.I6J64 1985

— — — —. "The CIA: Controlling the Quiet Option." *Foreign Policy,* no. 39, summer 1980: 143-153. LRS80-21642

Discusses CIA covert actions and the call for greater legislative control of intelligence agencies.

— — — —. "Legislative Reform of Intelligence Policy." *Polity,* v. 17, spring 1985: 549-573. LRS85-5560

"In this article Professor Johnson provides an account of the attempts of Congress to develop a legal framework for enforcing the intelligence agencies' accountability. Full accountability remains elusive. For given the absence of a consensus on the legal and moral status, or even the necessity, of covert operations abroad, Congress is not able to agree on how much accountability it should require and how best that may be ensured."

Laqueur, Walter. "The Future of Intelligence." *Society,* v. 23, Nov.-Dec. 1985: 3-11. LRS85-11048

Evaluates aspects of U.S. intelligence policy, including the congressional role and the role of intelligence in the conduct of foreign policy.

Latimer, Thomas K. "U.S. Intelligence and the Congress." *Strategic Review,* v. 7, summer 1979: 47-56. LRS79-13768

"Congress has gained an expanded role in overseeing the intelligence activities of the government. Congressional attention centers upon five concerns: investigation, oversight, budget review, quality of analysis and legislation. By establishing guidelines and by overseeing the activities, budget requests and quality of assessments of the intelligence services, Congress ensures that intelligence analysts adequately anticipate crises and that their assessments reach the levels of policy formulation."

Leyton-Brown, David. "The Role of Congress in the Making of Foreign Policy." *International Journal,* v. 38, winter 1982-1983: 59-76. LRS82-18535

"During the 1970s, Congress acted on a number of fronts to reverse publicly the decisions of the president and the foreign policy experts of the executive branch, to impose prohibitions and restrictions on future actions, and to mandate new policy behavior. The many areas of congressional activism included military activity, arms sales, intelligence operations, trade, aid, nuclear proliferation, human rights, and surveillance of executive agreements."

Lindsay, John V. "Watching Secret Operations." *New York Times,* Aug. 5, 1987: A27. LRS87-10367

Former member of Congress contends that "after the Bay of Pigs it became evident that joint oversight in Congress was needed."

Lobel, Jules. "Covert War and Congressional Authority: Hidden War and Forgotten Power." *University of Pennsylvania Law Review,* v. 134, June 1986: 1035-1110. LRS86-9913

"Article describes the historical development of letters of marque and reprisal and explains why the Constitution should treat modern covert warfare as it treated private wars in the eighteenth century . . . Explores the historical, doctrinal, and policy rationales for placing the power over privately conducted warfare in the hands of Congress. . . . Discusses recent congressional efforts to gain oversight over covert operations and concludes that Congress may not delegate its authority over paramilitary operations to the executive."

Luttwak, Edward N. "How to Administer Covert Operations." *New York Times,* Nov. 17, 1986: A21. LRS86-14254

Senior Fellow at the Center for Strategic and International Studies contends that "the CIA would not have fumbled in Nicaragua and in the Iran deal . . . . The problem is twofold: the CIA will not now act without permission from Congressional intelligence committees, and Congress has failed to develop practicable oversight procedures and safeguards. The result is paralysis. No official of the CIA in his senses would knowingly participate in a secret operation unless duly authorized by Congress, lest he find himself answering charges and possibly going to jail as a result of future investigations."

McCormick, James M. Smith, Steven S. "The Iran Arms Sales

and the Intelligence Oversight Act of 1980." *PS*, v. 20, winter 1987: 29-37. LRS87-1229

Reviews the 1980 Intelligence Oversight Act, considers "the ambiguities of its application highlighted in the Iran-Contra arms deal, and discusses the possible consequences of this episode for the formal and informal role of Congress in intelligence oversight."

The Military Intelligence Community. Edited by Gerald W. Hopple and Bruce W. Watson. Boulder, Colo., Westview Press, 1986. 298 p. (Westview special studies in military affairs) LRS86-10639

Partial contents.—The defense intelligence community, by J. Thompson Strong.—Law and intelligence, by Morton H. Halperin.—The intelligence community and the news media, by George H. Quester.—Congressional oversight: form and substance, by Gary J. Schmitt.

The Missing Dimension: Governments and Intelligence Communities in the Twentieth Century. Edited by Christopher Andrew and David Dilks. Urbana, University of Illinois Press, 1984. 300 p. UB250.M57 1984

Oseth, John M. *Regulating U.S. Intelligence Operations: A Study in Definition of the National Interest.* Lexington, Ky., University Press of Kentucky, 1985. 236 p. JK468.I6O84 1985

"Perspectives on U.S. Intelligence." *Washington Quarterly*, v. 6, summer 1983: 15-48. LRS83-10203

A "cluster of articles which provide widely varying perspectives and judgments on the character of American intelligence in the 1980s."

Contents.—Congress and Intelligence Oversight, by B. Goldwater.—Intelligence Oversight: Has Anything Changed? by A. Karalekas.—The Substance and the Rules, by A. Codevilla.—The Limits of Warning, by R. Brody.

President's Special Review Board (U.S.) Report. Washington, The Board, for sale by the Supt. of Docs., G.P.O., 1987. 1 v. (ca. 304 p. in various pagings.) LRS87-627

Report of the "Tower Commission."

This report examines the operation of the National Security Council and also focuses on the "Iran/Contra matter."

Partial contents.—Organizing for national security.—Arms transfers to Iran, diversion, and support for the contras.—What was wrong.—The Iran/Contra affair: a narrative.—The NSC staff and the contras.

Pyle, Christopher H. Pious, Richard M. *The President, Congress, and the Constitution: Power and Legitimacy in American Politics.* New York, Free Press, 1984. 433 p.
KF5050.P94 1984

Report of the Congressional Committees Investigating the Iran-Contra Affair with Supplemental, Minority, and Additional Views. Washington, G.P.O., 1987. 690 p. (Report, Senate, 100th Congress, 1st session, no 100-216 Report, House, 100th Congress, 1st session, no. 100-433) LRS 87-9200

"Union Calendar no. 77"

"The common ingredients of the Iran and Contra policies were secrecy, deception, and disdain for the law. A small group of senior officials believed that they alone knew what was right. They viewed knowledge of their actions by others in the Government as a threat to their objectives. They told neither the Secretary of State, the Congress nor the American people of their actions."

Includes recommendations and extensive minority views on the congressional role in managing covert operations.

Richelson, Jeffrey. *The U.S. Intelligence Community.* Cambridge, Mass., Ballinger Pub. Co., 1985. 358 p.
JK468.I6R53 1985

Solomon, Gerald B. Fein, Bruce. "A Tight Plug on Intelligence Leaks." *New York Times,* June 10, 1987: A31. LRS87-10260

Member of the House Foreign Affairs Committee and minority research director for the House Committee probing the Iran-Contra Affair asserts that the creation of a joint congressional committee to oversee the intelligence community "would strengthen oversight and allay apprehensions among foreign intelligence agencies and operatives that covert cooperation with the C.I.A. and other components of the American intelligence community would be publicly exposed."

Szulc, Tad. "Putting Back the Bite in the CIA." *New York Times Magazine,* Apr. 6, 1980: 28-29, 33, 62, 64. LRS80-2294

"In the wake of the CIA's failures and illegal acts, Congress put a brake on its freewheeling ways. Now, as feelings of U.S. vulnerability mount, there is a drive to unleash the agency again."

Treverton, Gregory F. "Covert Action and Open Society." *Foreign Affairs,* v. 65, summer 1987: 995-1014. LRS87-9176

"The Iran/Contra affair raises some questions: Should the United States attempt major covert operations at all? In what circumstances, and—crucially—how, if at all, can these secret operations be made to square with the requirements of governance in an open democracy?

Turner, Stansfield. "Covert Common Sense: Don't Throw the CIA Out with the Ayatollah." *Washington Post,* Nov. 23, 1986: D1-D2. LRS86-14253

Former CIA director comments on congressional oversight of intelligence activities. Contends that "we must have congressional oversight of our intelligence activities, especially covert operations, which really amount to clandestine foreign policy. But oversight will work only if there is a high degree of mutual trust between Congress and the White House.

―――――. "Intelligence: The Right Rules," by Stansfield Turner and George Thibault. *Foreign Policy,* no. 48, fall 1982: 122-138. LRS82-11378

"The United States cannot afford to ignore once again the inherent conflict between secrecy and democracy. A consistent and stable system of controls and oversight for intelligence is needed, for the sake of intelligence professionals who have been trying to do their jobs while never knowing exactly what they were authorized to do, and for the sake of the American people who discovered a few years ago that their blind trust in the intelligence community had been unwise."

U.S. Commission on CIA activities within the United States.

Report to the President. Washington, 1975. 299 p. LRS75-7220
"Rockefeller Commission"

Among areas covered by the Rockefeller Commission were supervision and control of the CIA.

Walden, Jerrold L. "The CIA: A Study in the Arrogation of Administrative Powers." *George Washington Law Review,* v. 39, Oct. 1970: 66-101. LRS71-2079

Explores the origins of the Central Intelligence Agency, the congressional purpose in creating it, the sources of its powers, and the adequacy of supervision over its activities.

Wayne, E. A. "Tightening the Reins on U.S. Intelligence." *Christian Science Monitor,* Nov. 13, 1987: 1, 32. LRS87-10262

"The Iran-Contra affair has spawned Senate sentiment for bills that would ensure tough congressional oversight of covert activities.

Weiner, Tim. "Pentagon's Secret Funds Under Fire." *Philadelphia Inquirer,* Mar. 13, 1987: 1A, 5A. LRS87-7158

"The Pentagon is facing a growing congressional clamor for facts about the super-secret 'black budget,' that portion of its military and intelligence programs that are classified. Two bills introduced . . . would compel the Department of Defense to reveal the size and nature of black programs, which are now hidden from congressional scrutiny."

Whited, Roberta. *Leaks: Concern and Control.* Columbia, School of Journalism, University of Missouri, 1976. 6 p. (Missouri. University. Freedom of Information Center. Report no. 356) LRS76-10794

Discusses current controversies involving the unauthorized disclosure of official secrets growing out of the congressional investigation of the intelligence community.

Wise, David. "Is Anybody Watching the CIA?" *Inquiry* (San Francisco), v. 1, Nov. 27, 1979: 17.21. LRS78-22091

"A first-hand examination of the congressional oversight committees raises a disturbing question: does oversee now mean overlook?"